THE Youth Worker's
G·u·i·d·e
to
CREATIVE
Bible Study

REVISED & EXPANDED

One of the most creative minds in youth ministry today is Karen Dockrey. Her many years of experience as a youth Bible study leader, her understanding of adolescence, and her unique ability to communicate biblical truth to teenagers makes her the ideal person to teach us about youth Bible study.

Lynn H. Pryor, Biblical Studies Designer, LifeWay

A must-have for every youth worker's library, *Youth Worker's Guide to Creative Bible Study* puts exciting and creative ideas for this week's Bible study at the fingertips of the youth workers who want to involve their group members in discovering the truth of God's Word.

Bryan Hall, Youth/College Minister, Woodlawn Baptist Church, Austin, TX

Karen combines integrity, methodology, creativity, and practicality into one incredible package. Few books are important enough to keep giving away. I sure wish I could remember who borrowed my copy.

Allen Jackson, Professor of Youth Education, New Orleans Baptist Seminary

If boredom is the enemy of learning, Karen Dockrey's book drives boredom out the door and invites learning to pervade your class. You'll catch youth by surprise with the wake-'em-up methods on these pages. As a Christian educator and curriculum writer I regularly turn to it for fresh ideas and methods.

Walter Norvell, doctoral candidate in Christian education, curriculum writer

For the past fifteen years, I have led seminars and conferences across the country to equip adults who work with teenagers. Wherever I go, I say, If you can only afford one book, this is it: Karen Dockrey's *Youth Workers' Guide To Creative Bible Study.* I use Karen's ideas in my conference leading, in curriculum writing, and in teaching my own Sunday Bible study classes. Karen's book has saved me many hours by providing instructions, an index of methods, and invaluable tips at the beginning of each chapter.

Brenda Harris, LifeWay curriculum writer and conference leader

Wow! This comprehensive book is like a fun trip to a giant shopping mall. It's loaded with ideas, tips, and activities of all shapes and sizes. Wander through the chapters and pick and and choose what's best for your group. It's a useful tool I'll be using for my own Sunday school and youth group.

Alfred Lu, Canadian high school teacher and Bible study curriculum writer

Karen Dockrey's *Youth Worker's Guide to Creative Bible Study* has been one of the most requested books by youth workers in my conferences across North Carolina. When workers with youth read through her methods, it is evident that Karen has been there. She writes not only as an educator but mainly as a practitioner, one who teaches every Sunday in her own church.

Philip W. Stone, Youth Consultant, Baptist State Convention of North Carolina

The warmth and insight with which Karen writes gives evidence of her authentic love for young people. If you want to improve as a Bible teacher, this book will help you succeed. It is a teacher-friendly resource that constantly urges me to become a better teacher. To teach youth effectively, workers must understand teenagers and encourage not only Bible knowledge but also a growing faith in Jesus Christ. This book shows you how. Its innumerable suggestions are practical, and each suggestion is undergirded by sound educational principles.

Gary Gramling, Associate Professor, Howard Payne University

Youth Worker's Guide to Creative Bible Study is *the* definitive book for involving youth in the study and application of God's Word. I believe it is a must for the library of any youth worker who is serious about guiding their youth to discover how the Bible impacts daily life. That book stays on my credenza, next to my computer. I use it for writing, and for planning for Sunday School every week.

Ozzie Ingram, Dean of the Weekend College, Dallas Baptist University

I am constantly looking for helps for older children's workers. I gladly promote Karen's *Youth Worker's Guide to Creative Bible Study* in all my conferences for older children's workers and for preteen workers. I already recommend this book to writers and editors of preteen and youth materials, and to anyone in the church who works with preteens or youth.

Judy Latham, Biblical Studies Designer, Older Children's Team, LifeWay

I'm especially interested in the beginning section that spells out the seemingly hundreds of teaching methods used by Jesus. Indeed, Jesus really *is* the master teacher; and knowing that he used dozens of styles, depending upon the setting, the time, the audience, etc., helps me do the same. Your insights and words cause me to think, "Yeah, that's exactly the way it is with my youth."

Rita McCoy, R.N, American Baptist youth worker, Richmond IN

You know what will sell this book? Karen Dockrey's name. People know what she does is trustworthy biblically and it works. You don't have to wonder about it. . .I'm delighted the book may find new life!

Jane Vogel, editor

I think the *Youth Worker's Guide to Creative Bible Study* is excellent because it's so easy. I can give it to brand new youth workers, and they know just what to do in class after they read it. Karen also gives the pluses and minuses for each kind of method. I tell every youth worker they need this book.

Barbara Warfield, youth specialist

™Youth Worker's
G·u·i·d·e
to
CREATIVE
Bible Study

REVISED & EXPANDED

Karen Dockrey

BROADMAN
& HOLMAN
PUBLISHERS

Nashville, Tennessee

Published by Broadman & Holman Publishers, Nashville, Tennessee
Acquisitions and Development Editor: Leonard G. Goss
Page Design and Typesetting: TF Designs, Mt. Juliet, Tennessee
Dewey Decimal Classification: 220
Subject Heading: BIBLE STUDY AND TEACHING/YOUTH WORK
Library of Congress Card Catalog Number: 98-45976

Unless otherwise noted, Scripture quotations are from the Holy Bible,
New International Version, © copyright 1973, 1978, 1984.
Other versions are marked NASB, the New American Standard Bible,
© Copyright The Lockman Foundation, 1960, 1962, 1963, 1968,
1971, 1972, 1973, 1975, 1977, 1995;
NKJV, New King James Version, copyright © 1979, 1980, 1982,
Thomas Nelson, Inc., Publishers.
GNB, Good News Bible: The Bible in Today's English Version,
© American Bible Society 1966, 1971, 1976; used by permission.

Library of Congress Cataloging-in-Publication Data
Dockrey, Karen, 1955–
    The youth worker's guide to creative Bible study / by Karen
        Dockrey.—Rev. and expanded ed.
        p. cm.
    Includes index.
    ISBN 0-8054-1837-7
    1. Bible—Study and teaching. 2. Church group work with youth.
    3. Christian education of teenagers. I. Title.
BS600.2.D621999
220'.071'2—dc21

                                                            98-45976
                                                            CIP

                            4 5 03 02 01

Contents

Involvement activities don't come before or after the
serious Bible study—they are the Bible study.

The book can make your design of an involvement Bible study easier or
help you discover an alternate method if your curriculum has a weak step. As
you look for a teaching method, notice that the methods are in alphabetical
order within chapters. They are also listed in the index. And the chapter
themes will help you find the type of activity your students need. Let God
guide you to his best choices for your students.

Imitate Jesus' pattern of teaching—for learning that lasts.

Help youth be safe, smart, and spiritual as they move toward the
Savior.

Display attitudes and actions that enhance youth's receptiveness
to Bible truth and to letting the Bible change their lives.

Part 2: Bible Study Methods

Make Bible reading stick with over a dozen ways to read Scripture with interest and meaning.

Play meaningful games that keep students reading and rereading
their Bibles.

Use questions to invite discussion as students move from Bible discovery to Bible understanding.

Challenge with writing projects, word puzzles, drawing methods, and other actions that help students solidify their Bible understanding on paper.

Jump-start your discussion with these tried-and-true ways to get students to talk about the Bible.

Incorporate these methods and be amazed at the depth of spiritual insight youth can express through them.

Use music to enhance Bible memory, convey Bible moods, and make Bible application apparent for all students, even those who avoid music.

Set up projects that help teenagers dig out Bible truth and express it in a form they'll remember.

Create experiences that help teenagers apply what they've learned. Jesus taught much of his truth through experience.

Try these fun and lively ways to make memorization painless and effective.

Part 3: Put It All Together

Listen in as youth teachers get advice for their top concerns in this question-and-answer section.

Spell R.E.A.D.Y. to get ready to lead youth Bible study.

Use a different method each time you divide youth into small groups to keep interest and bridge youth friendships.

Announcements happen every week. Keep your kids listening by varying the way you communicate.

Variety makes learning intriguing. So just as you vary any other teaching factor, vary your chair arrangements. Youth will come in wondering what the chairs mean.

See a method in your curriculum that you're not sure how to do? Remember a method from this book but can't remember which chapter it's in? This listing helps you find both.

Introduction

Why read this book? It demonstrates over 350 ways to guide teenagers to study and live the Bible.

As a teacher of youth, do you feel caught between entertaining your students and staying serious about the Bible? The good news is that serious Bible study can be the most engaging activity of all:

- As teenagers participate in their own learning, they find more than entertainment—they find true-to-life answers, answers they seek with a passion.
- As teenagers accept the invitation to look directly in their own Bibles, they find more than interesting information—they find God's guide to life.
- As teenagers do their own digging, they find more than treasure—they meet God the Father, Son, and Holy Spirit.

How wonderful each Sunday morning would be if each teenage student participated, searched the Bible they brought, and dug for the treasure of knowing God!

Yeah, right! I do well if I can keep my teenagers from hitting each other over the head with their Bibles, if they bring their Bibles in the first place. You're dreaming!

Solid and fascinating youth Bible studies are not a dream—they become reality each time a teacher equips youth to study the Bible. This book is designed to show teachers just how to do this. It's not an ivory tower book but one written by a youth worker with twenty-five years of experience teaching every age, stage, and temperament of teenagers in church. The ideas aren't instant solutions, but with steady love and persistent dedication teachers can let God teach through them.

The Youth Worker's Guide to Creative Bible Study includes actions that get kids into the Bible the minute they walk in the door and keep them there through motivation steps, examination steps and application steps. These ideas help you use your church's curriculum well or develop your own Bible studies. Here is some of what you'll find:

- Thirty ways Jesus taught
- Bible learning games and Bible reading strategies that hook youth's interest
- Creative questioning, paper-and-pencil activities, talk starters, and more that guide youth to dig into what the Bible meant and what it means to them today
- Art, drama, music, project ideas, and life application strategies that guide youth to apply the Bible to life
- Bible memory processes that hide God's Word in youth's hearts so they can live it wherever they are
- Tips for youth Bible study preparation
- Thirty-two ways to divide into groups or form teams
- Thirty ways to make announcements
- A dozen ways to group your chairs
- A full index so you can find the method you're looking for

All of these ideas are woven together by delighting in youth and letting God's very loving Spirit guide you. You'll find nearly 300 fully developed ideas and 130 seed ideas to make Bible study with youth delightful. Come embark on the adventure of life-changing Bible study.

Part One

❦

How to Teach

Chapter One

❦

What Makes a Quality Bible Study?

Involvement is the key to learning that lasts.

When's the last time you stole Bible learning from your teenagers? You wouldn't do this intentionally, but consider that the one who does the talking, searching, doodling, and presenting is the one who learns. How often have you reserved this privilege for yourself by studying during the week and then pouring out your knowledge to your pupils? Discover how to give this privilege back to your students by involving them with the Bible.

I don't see why we can't just teach the Bible. Why do we have to do all this method stuff? I'm for serious Bible study. Youth should be too.

For too many teachers, "serious Bible study" means lecture and verse by verse "what-does-this-mean-to-you" Bible study. These methods are valid, but they are not the only ways to be serious about Bible study.

Teach as Jesus Taught

I can think of no more serious teacher than Jesus Christ himself. Look at the variety of ways he taught, and invite him to show you how to teach as he taught:

1. *Jesus invited others to talk.* "Who do people say that I am?" Jesus invited talking by moving from general to specific, from others' opinions to one's own. Perhaps this helped people grow comfortable before addressing tougher questions. Jesus then asked the personal question: "Who do you say I am?" (Matt. 16:13, 15).

2. *Jesus asked questions.* Sometimes Jesus used questions to help people draw conclusions, such as when he spoke with the rich ruler about eternal life (Luke 18:18–29). Other times Jesus used questions to correct thinking, as when he talked with religious leaders about authority (Matt.

21:23–27). Jesus did not answer his own questions. Instead he used questions to lead his listeners toward truth.

3. *Jesus moved from the simple to the complex.* When Jesus talked with the woman at the well he began with water, compared that water to eternal life, and finally explained the Messiah (John 4:1–26).

4. *Jesus demonstrated the value of each person.* He spent time listening to and understanding people, regardless of their background. He went to their homes. He accepted Zacchaeus, the hated tax collector, when no one else would. Rather than judge him, Jesus let God's love transform him (Luke 19:2–10).

5. *Jesus compared spiritual truth to everyday experiences.* Jesus frequently spoke in parables. These "earthly stories with heavenly meaning" made spiritual truth clear: "The kingdom of God . . . is like a mustard seed" (Luke 13:19).

6. *Jesus used assignments and challenges.* He sent the disciples out in pairs to heal the sick and proclaim the kingdom of God. Notice the specificity of his instructions in Luke 10:1–12. He later challenged his followers to share his gospel with the world (Matt. 28:18–20).

7. *Jesus taught by life example.* He served by washing his disciples' feet (John 13:1–7). He taught baptism by being baptized (Matt. 3:13–17). He respected people by taking time for children (Matt. 19:13–15). He saw the good in each person by talking with ignored people (John 4:9).

8. *Jesus explained his examples.* After washing his disciples' feet, Jesus urged his disciples to express the same loving action (John 13:12–17).

9. *Jesus gave evidence to end doubt.* Doubt is frequently a plea for solid answers. So rather than scold Thomas for his religious questions, Jesus gave him the evidence he needed to believe (John 20:24–28).

10. *Jesus quoted Scripture (Bible memory).* Jesus defeated Satan's temptation, and Satan's improper use of Scripture, with correctly used Bible quotations (Matt. 4:1–11).

11. *Jesus expressed emotion.* He wept upon discovering Lazarus's death (John 11:35–36). He showed anger toward the money changers in the temple (Mark 11:15–17). He agonized over his approaching crucifixion (Luke 22:44).

12. *Jesus responded to emotion.* Jesus responded to his mother's worry by explaining why he stayed in the temple (Luke 2:49). Jesus comforted his disciples by assuring them he would prepare a place for them (John

14:1–3). At the Last Supper Jesus tempered Peter's overconfidence by telling him what to do after failure (Luke 22:32).

13. *Jesus forgave.* After Peter denied Jesus, Jesus forgave Peter and challenged him to feed his sheep (John 21:16).

14. *Jesus prayed for himself and his students.* With tenderness, compassion, and understanding of their challenges, Jesus prayed for his disciples, for all his followers, and for himself (John 17).

15. *Jesus affirmed correct conclusions.* When the high priest asked if Jesus was the Son of God, Jesus agreed that he was (Matt. 26:64).

16. *Jesus spent time with his students.* He called twelve people to be his closest disciples (Mark 1:17–20). He talked with them while they traveled (Mark 11:20–25), rested with them (Mark 6:30–31), shared the Last Supper with them (Mark 14:12–26), and more. He also spent time teaching others who were interested in him (Mark 6:34–44).

17. *Jesus gave object lessons.* Jesus used a coin to teach about taxes (Mark 12:16–17). He used the stones of magnificent buildings to explain the intensity of the end of the age (Mark 13:1–4). He used a fig tree to illustrate both faith and his return (Matt. 21:21, 24:30–36).

18. *Jesus used waiting and silence.* Jesus calmed a potential catastrophe by waiting for would-be stoners to answer his question about sin (John 8:1–11). Jesus was silent before his accusers, perhaps realizing that words would do no good in that situation (Luke 23:9).

19. *Jesus promised the power of God.* In John 14:1–3 Jesus told his believers they could depend on him to prepare a place for them in heaven. In Acts 1:8 he promised the power of the Holy Spirit.

20. *Jesus gently but firmly corrected misunderstandings about God.* He helped his disciples see that children weren't a bother to serious religion but a demonstration of it (Matt. 19:13–15). He rebuked his disciples when they spoke or acted wrongly (Mark 8:33).

21. *Jesus demonstrated truth.* Jesus walked on water, which showed God's power over nature and fear (Matt. 14:22–33). He ate with sinners, which showed God wants closeness with everyone (Matt. 9:11–12).

22. *Jesus asked people to express their needs.* Even though God already knew what people needed, Jesus asked them to voice their need (Matt. 20:29–34). This voicing led people to trust God to meet those needs.

23. *Jesus gave the bad news and then the good news.* After describing the woes of cities who had not repented, Jesus explained the good that would happen for those who did turn to him (Matt. 11:20–30).

24. *Jesus gave specific instructions.* After his resurrection and before he ascended to heaven, Jesus gave specific directions about where to wait for the Holy Spirit and what to do when he arrived (Acts 1:4–9).

25. *Jesus used case studies.* He explained righteousness to the Pharisees with a story about two people in church (Luke 18:9–14). Another story began "There was a man who had two sons . . ." (Luke 15:11).

26. *Jesus drew and wrote.* Jesus wrote in the sand while waiting for the accusers to decide which one of them had no sin (John 8:6–8).

27. *Jesus listened and encouraged others to listen.* As a twelve-year-old he himself learned by listening to teachers in the temple (Luke 2:46). He reminded his followers to listen to understand (Matt. 15:10, 11:15, 13:18).

28. *Jesus made divine demands clear.* He commanded demons to leave innocent people (Luke 4:35). He expected his followers to obey God (Luke 14:28). He explained that going to church wasn't enough, that we must let God change our everyday actions and attitudes (Matt. 23:27–28).

29. *Jesus admitted what he didn't know.* Jesus told his disciples that only God the Father knows the day and hour of Jesus' return (Mark 13:32).

30. *Jesus used lecture very occasionally.* The Sermon on the Mount (Matt. 5–7) is the one long lecture of Jesus recorded in our Bible.

No matter how Jesus taught, he guided his pupils to discover, understand, and live his truth. He involved them in the learning experience.

What implications do Jesus' methods have for your teaching? How might you teach more like Jesus taught?

Search Matthew, Mark, Luke, John, and Acts 1:1–11 to study the way Jesus taught. Focus on Jesus as you plan Bible studies for your students.

Identify Good Bible Study Methods

I want to teach like Jesus did. But I don't want to end up entertaining my students rather than leading them to study the Bible. What's the difference between fun activities and solid Bible study?

Fun itself is not the measure of a good Bible study method; student involvement with the Bible is. When students read, search, talk about, and make presentations on the Bible, they learn. Even more importantly they connect to God, the author of the Bible. Entertaining youth is boring and mean-ingless; encountering Jesus Christ is true delight. Discover and use teaching methods that get youth to open their own Bibles, dig deeply, and know its author with fascination and commitment.

The "Rationale" section at the beginning of each methods chapter (4 through 13) shows how the ideas in that chapter keep youth learning without losing interest and without empty entertainment. In general, a quality Bible study method includes at least one of these four characteristics:

1. *Includes Bible reading.* A good Bible study method requires youth to read the Bible passage at least once. If students' Bibles aren't open, they can't be doing Bible study.

2. *Discovers Bible facts.* A good Bible study method sends youth to the Bible for answers. When youth play Bible Jeopardy, they must dig hard in their Bibles to question an answer. When youth summarize a Bible truth in four words or less, they must study the passage to do so.

3. *Explains Bible facts.* A good Bible study method leads to Bible under-standing. As youth write a job description for the Holy Spirit, they learn how he works. As students present a modern-day parable, they under-stand how to live as a citizen of the kingdom of God.

4. *Applies the Bible to life.* A good Bible study method guides students to live what they learned. Students can give Bible answers all day, but those answers do little good if students don't practice them in daily life. When youth actually resist a temptation, then you know that the Bible study on temptation was a good one.

As youth read, discover, explain, and apply, encourage them to use all of their senses. The more senses they use, the longer they'll remember what they studied. Find opportunities for youth not only to hear Bible truth but to *see it* (poster, visual, chalkboard), *touch it* (sculpture, object lessons, writing), *say it* (drama, 60-second speeches, sharing ideas), and *live it* (comfort a depressed friend, telephone a newcomer to invite her to the event).

Include Four Elements for Quality Bible Study

I feel better about trying new Bible study methods, but I'm not sure how to put a Bible study together. How do I arrange it?

A good Bible study is more than a conglomeration of methods. It's a mean-ingful arrangement of actions that flows from Bible fact discovery to Bible application. Most Bible study curriculum will arrange this flow for you.

When it doesn't, or when you're designing your own study, include four steps:

1. *Find a creative way to read the Bible passage.* Begin by giving students a reason to read the Bible passage. Perhaps you'll challenge them to find the answer to a question or the names of certain people. Maybe they'll act out the passage, using the Bible as their script. Or maybe they'll play a learning game that requires them to read the Bible to find the answers. In any case, motivate youth to open their Bibles.

2. *Get the facts.* Without examining the facts, youth have no basis on which to make comments or draw conclusions. Guide youth to discover Bible facts with a method like those described in chapters 5, 6, or 7. Perhaps they'll find a question under their chair that guides each to a different fact. Maybe they'll use their Bibles to place facts in order. Maybe they'll create quizzes for each other to give double learning—while writing the questions and while answering.

3. *Understand the facts.* Guide your students to understand the facts they discover with a method from chapters 6 through 12. Perhaps they'll pretend to be a Bible character, such as the king who threw Daniel in the lions' den, writing the passage from Daniel's viewpoint. Or they'll demonstrate sanctification by shaping it with clay. Maybe they'll draw a before and after cartoon on the difference sanctification makes. Bible understanding has two elements: (1) what the Bible facts meant to those in Bible times, and (2) what the Bible facts mean to us today.

4. *Apply the facts.* Close with a step that guides youth to commit to live Bible truth. Bible knowledge means little if it never transforms lives. See application methods in chapters 11 through 13, and scattered through chapters 4 through 10. Perhaps your students will write and mail a letter showing compassion. Or they'll plan to request forgiveness from a family member. Or they'll choose to listen exclusively to Christian music to obey Philippians 4:8.

As you prepare and teach, you may find that steps overlap. Your Bible reading method may get kids asking questions about the facts in the passage. The fact method may guide students to tell how that truth has worked in their lives. This is the way it should be—a meaningful flow rather than sharply defined steps.

Involvement: For Learning That Lasts

So what does all this mean for my class?

Jesus wants to work through you to teach his truth. Ask his guidance as you enjoy and cherish this honor. The ultimate goal of Bible study is to involve students with God's Word so they will trust him as Savior and follow him as Lord. Guide youth to become involved with the Bible and thus with God with the following principles:

Involve rather than inform. Suppose you had climbed a mountain and wanted to convey to your students the exhilaration of reaching the top and the relief at discovering that the grueling work was really worth the effort. Would it be better to tell them about your climb or take them to the top of the mountain with you? Taking them to the top would take more time than saying, "The results are worth the climb." But which would youth remember? Which would impact their lives more deeply? Which would motivate them to climb the mountain again? It's the same with Bible study: the more youth do for themselves, the more meaningful their learning becomes.

Listen rather than lecture. The one who talks is the one who learns. When you ask questions and make assignments, let your students talk more than you do. Let them show and tell you the Bible truths they discover, rather than your showing and telling them. They'll find it easy to let lectures go in one ear and out the other, but they'll remember what they themselves say. Then they live what they commit to.

Direct rather than dictate. "Is this television program good for me?" "What is sin?" "How can I know the will of God?" Rather than tell youth what to do, guide them to Bible verses that address their questions. As youth make their own choices, they gain confidence in their ability to read and understand the Bible for themselves. And they grow close to God who authored the Bible.

Give variety rather than the same entrée. Youth, like persons of all ages, like to learn in different ways. As youth express Bible truths in ways that are comfortable to them, learning takes on special meaning. This doesn't mean singers must always sing to learn, but it means your class sings for the singers some of the time. Then you doodle for the doodlers the next week, dramatize Scripture for the actors, and discuss for the talkers. You choose methods for which all youth have to respond, even if it's not their favorite way. Rather than fret over who learns which way, relax with the truth that all youth learn best when you vary your methods—just like Jesus did.

Chapter 2

᯾

The Youth We Teach

*When we understand youth, they'll more likely
understand the Bible.*

Let everything you do in Bible study settings guide youth to feel *safe* and *smart* so they'll discover how to be *spiritual* and honor the *Savior*. Youth won't talk about spiritual things until they first discover that the people in the group cherish them and want to hear what they have to say. They won't discover how to be spiritual or choose to honor their Savior unless they see people around them doing so.

Youth's needs for safety, smartness, spirituality, and Savior-worship are easy to address with actions like welcoming every answer and giving attention to every youth. But you must be intentional. It's easy to give attention to the few who talk and assume the others are comfortable being quiet. Without meaning to, you communicate that your talkers are the spiritual ones and the others are just class members. There are no superspiritual teenagers; all matter equally to Jesus and to his kingdom. Each believer is a significantly gifted part of the body of Christ.

Deliberately cherish each student to demonstrate this body of Christ, that place where every believer has a critical role to play in the good of the whole. Recognize your mercy-givers and prophets, as well as your leaders. As Christian youth sense their place in your segment of the body of Christ, they eagerly explore how to be spiritual and how to honor God. They discover that the way they play cards on the church bus is as spiritually weighty as the way they speak their testimony before the church body. They find ways to show patience in their families, rather than just talk about how camp changed their lives.

Make It Safe

Every day youth are criticized and put down at school, work, play, and more. They need a haven from the cruelty of the world—a place where they can wonder and ask, without a hint of ridicule. Even without external ridicule, youth continually feel the tension between wanting to be competent, likeable, and Christian, but not quite making it. They want to try, but they fear failing—so make it easy to succeed in class by showing youth how to find the answers in the Bible passage you're studying. They want to be honest, but they fear being misunderstood—so understand and guide your students to understand each other. They want to be spiritual, but they aren't sure how—so affirm the ways they already honor God, and show them new ways. Provide a place where every question is respected and where the entire class works together to find God's answers to life's problems. This kind of loving gives youth a glimpse of God's kingdom. Here are four ways to make your class safe:

1. *Introduce three class rules:* (1) No slams—no one laughs at anyone else's comment, question, or concern. Instead we encourage each other toward Christlikeness (Heb. 10:24–25). (2) No such thing as a stupid question. We ask anything because no sincere question is a dumb question, and every comment makes sense when you hear what's really said (Matt. 7:7). (3) No talking when another talks. We do this so we can hear and cherish each other's pearls of wisdom (Eph. 4:13).

2. *Show interest in and listen to youth's everyday concerns.* "How was the math test?" "How are things at home?" "How's your love life?" "Tell me about that job interview." "What's happening in your friendships?" Then remember and ask again later. This communicates God's interest in every area of life.

3. *Include every student in all study steps.* If you have a hesitant student, let him practice privately with you while the others work on their activities; then call on him to present along with the others. If you have a youth who answers all the questions, gently prod her to listen to the others. If you have a youth with vision difficulties, make large-print posters so he can see the points. I once asked a struggling reader ahead of time if I could call on her to read. She said yes, so I did. The other class members worried that I was picking on her and told me so. "Is she a member of this class?" I asked. "Yes," they replied. "Then don't you think it's right that she do everything we do?" I questioned. "Well, yes, I guess you're right." My students didn't realize that skipping this student would make her feel left out. They thought skipping her would be kind. But once they understood, they gladly included her. She came

up weeks later and said, "Thanks. You're the only teacher who has ever let me read."

4. *Look past youth's masks.* At first your students will smile all the time, talk with heavenly lingo, deny struggles, and look perfectly fine. As they feel safe, they show both sad and happy times, talk with real words, conquer struggles, and face guilt head on by avoiding the wrong that causes it. They become free to grow in Christ.

Bring Out Each Student's Smartness

One basic reason students don't participate in class is because they don't want to look stupid in front of their peers. Even the school-smart may not know their Bible as well as their algebra. To keep from looking dumb, students will cut up, pretend they didn't hear the question, refuse to participate, or deliberately act stupid. Meet their need to look smart by structuring the session so they have success with the Bible. Begin with questions that come directly from the passages and proceed to questions that require deeper application. Show students that their attempts to answer spiritual questions will be accepted even when the answers are not quite right, and that people won't laugh when they try. As students look smart at church, they tend to trust God and his Book, citing him as the source of their competence. Use these strategies to help students be smart:

1. *Provide an answer source.* Guide students to open to the Bible passage before you ask questions or assign the learning strategy. Or direct them to the place in the student book that explains the assignment you give. Other answer sources include Bible dictionaries, concordances, charts, and maps. Answer sources help students discover new Bible knowledge, keep students from guessing or drawing on past knowledge, and help both hesitant and eager learners succeed because they know just where to look in their Bibles or the commentary for the answers. An example of how to give an answer source: "Look in 1 Timothy 6:1–10 to write three guidelines for how a Christian should use money."

2. *Notice success.* Youth will look to you to see if they got the right answer. Even when they know they're right, they'll discredit the answer if you don't welcome it. In one class a student answered that the end to Peter's timidity was the indwelling of the Holy Spirit. Another student then said that Peter stopped being timid about sharing Jesus when the Holy Spirit came. Both answers are exactly correct. But the teacher said, "Uh-huh" to the first student and an enthusiastic, "You are exactly right!" to the second. This teacher had

grown so used to the second student answering that she didn't even hear when the first one was correct. And the first youth wondered why the second copied her answer and got credit. Deliberately highlight the wisdom in each youth's answer to avoid this destructive mistake.

3. *Begin with the easier questions and move toward harder ones.* When Jesus talked with his disciples after his resurrection, he began by asking about their feelings: "Why are you troubled?" (Luke 24:38). He then showed them the answer to their question: his hands and feet. (Luke 24:39). He then asked another easy question: "Do you have anything here to eat?" (Luke 24:41). He ended by explaining deep spiritual truths (Luke 24:44–49). Imagine the disciples relaxing and opening their minds to spiritual truth as Jesus talked with them as recorded in Luke 24:36–49. Invite Jesus to guide you to teach similarly.

4. *Make your directions very specific.* Rather than instructing "Write the passage in your own words," say "Write the verse line by line leaving a blank line between each line. Then on the blank line, note situations that could happen today that are like the Bible event." When students know step by step how to study the Bible, they'll try it.

Highlight the Spiritual

Talking about spiritual things is hard. It requires students to reveal themselves and their very personal relationship (or lack of it) with God. To venture talking about such sacred things, students first have to feel safe and smart talking about simple things. They must see how the Bible relates to even the simplest worry and pleasure. They must have success with answering Bible questions and opportunities to explore how spiritual truth impacts life.

Once students begin to feel safe and smart, they risk sharing their beliefs, hopes, and dreams. We teachers must then, and with equal sensitivity, continue to cherish every contribution by every student. Once we communicate that a question or idea is stupid, students will close off again. Certainly some comments are less than profound, but even the most outrageous statement can lead to life-changing discovery. Treasure students' contributions with these affirmations: "Very good answer on a hard question;" "I can tell you're thinking about that one;" "You're seeing just what that passage teaches." The more students succeed with the Bible, the more they'll read and understand it at home.

As treasured students explore God and how best to serve him, they find answers to their questions. They discover that spirituality is seeing the world and relationships the way God does—and then living in harmony with that seeing. They invite the new girl to sit at their lunch table with the same holy commitment that leads them to church each Sunday. They discover that genuine smiles are the spiritual ones—so they let their faces communicate the care they feel. They discover that talking honestly with God empowers them to solve problems—so they frankly talk over everything with God, including how to involve the new girl in lunch table conversation. They find that guilt means not that they are bad but that they need to give attention to some parts of their lives—so they stop ignoring the other guy in the lunchroom.

Incorporate these ideas to encourage spiritual growth:

1. *Recognize that youth don't necessarily believe what they say.* They may be voicing a view they heard someone else say. They may be trying one of God's ideas to see how it works. Listen, understand, and gently guide them to compare what they say to what God's Word says. Let them discover and voice the truth. Consider these examples:

- Jason reacted against "Obey your parents" (Eph. 6:1a). Rather than "Who are you to question God's Word!" his teacher said, "You must have a good reason to react so strongly. Tell me why you feel that way." Honest discussion demonstrated that Jason's dad abused Jason's sister, and Jason's dad wanted Jason to keep it a secret. Jason rightly concluded that God would not want him to obey this request.

- Jeni spoke eloquently about being kind to people. But her actions outside of class showed that she actually ignored all but her chosen few friends. Her teacher, unconscious of this sinful pattern, refused to settle for standard answers and pushed Jeni to go deeper by asking: "With what words and actions do you show kindness—and how do you make certain you are kind to everyone, not just a few?" Friends in the class breathed a sigh of relief that Jeni might learn to be nicer.

2. *Present spirituality as a journey and a series of choices rather than something you have or don't have.* Too many youth see their salvation decision as the only decision they need to make for Jesus. Guide them to discover that they daily make decisions to honor or disgrace Jesus. They can talk kindly to a friend or slam her ideas. They can choose to redeem problems or get revenge. When the Holy Spirit nudges them with guilt, they can change the behavior that caused it or angrily ignore the guilt. They can talk with God to find out what to do with their sadness, or they can wallow in self-pity. They can encourage during games or win at all cost.

3. *Guide youth to embrace spirituality as a steering wheel, not a spare tire.* Youth frequently feel powerless. But they have the power of God at their fingertips. God wants to work through them—this is a revelation to most students. Help them live this revelation by deciding to draw on the Holy Spirit's power. Challenge them to watch each day for one good that God gives them opportunity to do, and then to do that good. Invite them to share the best part of their week and how they drew on God's power to make that happen. Invite them to share a temptation he helped them resist that week, and how he did it. This is not spiritual one-upmanship but encouraging one another to be decisive for Jesus.

4. *Continually point to Jesus as the source of power and solutions.* Youth are amazed that God himself lived on earth and knows what it's like going to school and dealing with girls. God in Jesus has been through it all, cares about them, and really does understand their worries (Heb. 4:14–16). Even better, he has the power to equip them.

5. *Show how to be spiritual by continually presenting new challenges.* One week challenge your students to dramatize the passage during class and then act out that truth at school. The next week invite them to write the passage in a letter they can deliver to a real person. Another time guide them to bring a contemporary Christian song that matches that week's Bible passage. Next guide them to write a letter of confession to God that they shred for privacy, as a picture that God takes care of our sins. Scan chapters 4 through 13 when you find yourself in a teaching rut.

Honor the Savior

Perhaps more than at any other time of life youth doubt themselves, feel lonely, worry that no one loves them, and wonder if their lives matter at all. Youth are sometimes well-adjusted, confident, reasonable, outgoing, and balanced. Other times they are moody, restless, rebellious, quarrelsome, withdrawn, sensitive, critical, and self-conscious. Move them toward the Savior in each Bible study to give them the Jesus-based security that is the foundation for managing all these times of life. Point them toward the Savior to grow their identity as children of God, to mature their faith, and to provide courage to do right no matter what mood they're in. Here are five ways to prompt youth to honor the Savior:

1. *Rejoice when youth ask faith questions.* When youth ask "How do I know God is even real?" push away your panic. Recognize questions as readiness for deeper faith. Then guide students to all the evidence God has given

for his existence: the orderliness of creation, the uniqueness of each person (if it was an automated process we'd all look alike), the Bible, the resurrection, and—the most powerful evidence of all—Jesus Christ.

The answers aren't easy, but the answers are there. Even more importantly, God himself is there to be the source of the answers to youth's questions. Youth ask many tough questions:

- Is God real?
- Does he care about me?
- How do I know what he wants?
- Why should I do right, if I get forgiven anyway?
- What's my place in this world?
- Do they like me?
- Which roles, tones of voice, and personality are best for me?
- How can I avoid being two-faced or hypocritical?
- How can I find love?
- What am I really good at?

God has the answers to all these questions. But know one important truth: you can't give these answers to youth. Youth must discover and embrace these answers for themselves. And as they study God's Word they will do exactly that.

2. *Notice the profound effect of youth's encountering God's Word.* Rather than trying to spoon-feed youth, let them feed on the milk and meat of God's Word. Prepare the learning experience and then watch as God teaches:

- Studying the Bible through **Bible Tic-Tac-Toe** (chapter 5) shows youth they can find the answers in the Bible all by themselves.
- Using the **Bible as Script** (chapter 4) helps students feel a part of the Bible action and recognize that the Bible is about people just like them.
- Studying the Bible through **Agree/Disagree** (chapter 8) helps students understand their beliefs by voicing every facet of God's powerful truth.
- **Clay Shaping** and **Tangram** (chapter 9) help students picture complex faith actions like sanctification. As they shape the pieces they discover what sanctification looks like and acts like. They know it when they see it.
- Reading the Bible through **Cued Reading** (chapter 4) shows youth that, even when they initially struggle with understanding certain Scripture verses, can find the answers.
- **Pretend You Are There** (chapter 12) guides students to feel part of the great cloud of witnesses who together please God with their actions and attitudes.

- **Music Memory** (chapter 13) makes faith personal because the song reminds youth to live the Scripture.
- Any talking method (chapter 8) helps God enhance the well-adjusted, confident, reasonable, outgoing, balanced side of students.
- **Spiritual Gift Saying** and **Affirmation by Name** (chapter 12) becomes a vehicle for God to tame the moody, restless, rebellious, quarrelsome, withdrawn, sensitive, critical, and self-conscious side by showing teens how loved they are.
- Studying any Old or New Testament passage helps students discover that the Bible relates to the past, present, and future. Passages like Mark 13 and Revelation show that even future events have present implications.
- **Role Play** (chapter 9) helps students discover and practice their role as a Christian, a family member, and the role they'd like to hold in the occupational world.
- Any teamwork (all chapters) helps students build bonds with other Christians, male and female, younger and older, alike and different. They develop respect and admiration for each other.
- **What If I Do/What If I Don't** (chapter 9) gives students courage to keep faith commitments by showing the disaster that comes if they don't keep God's commandments and the good that comes when they do. It enables students to "dress rehearse" decisions.

3. *Invite youth to share how Jesus is turning their moodiness into sensitivity, their restlessness into security, their quarrelsomeness into deliberate cooperation.* These short and simple testimonies show that Jesus' work is ongoing. He will empower youth to do right no matter how they feel or what curves life throws them. This is Holy Spirit work, and it's a great privilege to be a part of it. As they hear each other, kids can help each other discover that "God will meet all your needs according to his glorious riches in Christ Jesus" (Phil. 4:19).

4. *Launch younger youth into discovering God's truth for themselves.* Younger youth are just beginning to move from childhood to adulthood. You'll see glimpses of childishness followed by desperate pleas to be treated as mature. Let them know they are now old enough to begin finding their own faith answers and that those answers are found in a relationship with God himself. They can get to know God the Father, Son, and Holy Spirit by studying his Bible. Urge students to bring their own Bibles weekly so they can

mark and learn from them. But provide class Bibles to any who don't bring their own.

Because middle schoolers exhibit tremendous energy, give them active Bible study. Play human **Bible Tic-Tac-Toe** to learn the facts, dramatize the Scripture using youth's Bibles as their scripts to see how the facts fit together, and then turn a paper plate into a twelve-hour clock with a way that they'll please Jesus every hour of that day. During every step, focus middle schoolers on the Bible, conscious that interesting Bible study is the best discipline method. Because they're eager to get their team to win the Bible tic-tac-toe round they'll be less likely to pick at each other or show off. When the temptation pushes through anyway, remind them of the "no slam" rule and the fact that we all treasure each other (see the three class rules above in the "Make It Safe" section). Until middle schoolers can develop their own self-discipline, they need the safety of your limits, limits that say everybody participates and everybody matters.

See the good in middle schoolers to more easily tolerate their moodiness and movement. See their eagerness to be with each other but their fear at doing so. Use a different group-forming method every week to overcome this fear (see chapter 16). Recognize their great eagerness to find the right answers but their hesitance to show you that. Insist that everyone participate so it becomes cool to study the Bible. See their desire to do meaningful ministry, so you can show them what to say in a letter to a family with a tragedy. Give extra points for encouraging words during games to give students practice in the daily ministry of encouragement.

Middle schoolers are eager to live for Jesus, especially when their friends are living for Jesus. They are a tremendous tribute to the positive impact peer pressure can have. Let the class know you'd like to build a loving group, and guide them to do so by prodding compliments from the group as each member contributes Bible insight, by highlighting the spiritual gifts you see in each youth, and by affirming the times they show Jesus in their actions.

5. *Launch older youth into independent faith.* Older youth are closer to adulthood than to childhood. Many have grown physically as much as they are going to grow. But don't let their mature bodies fool you into thinking they have it all together. Though older students want independence, they need to know that it is OK to struggle, to wonder, to get help from others. Treat your senior highers as the mature people that they are, while allowing them the security of not being in charge. Share your own struggles to help free

senior highers to share their fears of growing up and making responsible choices. Then, together, find ways to make those choices. Explain that much of Christianity is deliberate loving action, motivated by obedience to Jesus.

Senior highers need you to go deep. Don't be afraid to delve into issues with no easy answers. You don't have to know all the answers—God does. So when students struggle to understand a tough issue, point them to God and his Word. Invite them to share their ideas with Bible support.

Senior highers need you to admit that the world is not perfect. Not all parents consider their children's needs. Not all bosses are fair. Not all Christians act like Christians. This imperfect world is countered by a very perfect Savior and Guide, Jesus Christ. Emphasize that obeying Jesus is the best alternative to the inconsistency of this world. Suggest that students focus on the obedient Christians and notice good works, rather than become discouraged by the opposite.

Senior highers want to do meaningful ministry. Respond to their ideas, help them determine motive and purpose, and guide them through the detail work that makes ministry successful. Help them word their cards, time their phone calls, go to the funeral home. Cultivate the habit of daily ministry by brainstorming ways to minister at work and school. Apprentice them by inviting them along as you do ministry. Give models for mentoring younger youth.

Interestingly, older students tend to be more open to activities some classify as "babyish" (play clay, acting, putting the truth into one sentence). They will amaze you with the depth of spiritual insight they express in these simple-on-the-surface activities.

Both middle schoolers and senior highers need your loving attention. They'll want your pride when they resist temptation, your prayer for their relationships, your help with their decisions. As you advise them, do more listening than talking and more pointing to Bible verses than giving pat answers. Make it a point to arrive early for Bible study, and be ready so you can chat as students arrive.

All in Jesus' Name

Let the Bible do for youth what God designed it to do: to prompt them to understand him, live for him, and love his people. Let the Bible show youth how to solve friendship struggles or manage a school challenge. Let the Bible answer students' very important questions like "Why doesn't God talk out loud?" and "How do I please him?" Let the Bible show students why their feelings of confusion and anger make sense. Then let the Bible show them the paths out of that confusion and anger.

The Bible is intriguing, need-meeting, and life-changing. God, its Author, gives youth the safety, smartness, spirituality, and Savior focus they crave. Help students see this by consciously showing how each passage applies to life, answers a life question, explains God, treasures us, or makes it easier to love and trust God.

Chapter 3

✺

Ten Commandments for Guiding a Youth Bible Study

How you use methods is as important as using methods.

A good Bible-teaching method involves students in the Bible. Our goal is youth's spiritual growth through Bible learning, not simply using methods for methods' sake. So each week find at least one way to better represent Jesus Christ as you teach. Following these commandments will help.

I. Thou Shalt Teach with Enthusiasm and Expectation

If you like Bible study, your students will tend to like it also. If you present a method with interest and delight, students will participate and like it. But if you say, "This was in the book, and I know you will think it childish and dumb" your students will think it childish and dumb. Expect great discovery based on Bible truths. Youth will sense your expectation and fulfill it.

II. Thou Shalt Let Your Students Do Their Own Bible Study

Refuse to steal Bible learning from your teenagers by studying during the week and then pouring out your knowledge for your pupils. Instead, let them do the searching, digging, and discovering. They can let your teaching go in one ear and out the other, but they will remember what they themselves discover, speak, and struggle over. Guide their learning by choosing a few methods each week that involve students in meaningful Bible searching of a single Bible passage. This involvement is the key to learning that lasts. *Important*: Choose methods that include everyone. Avoid methods that a few students do while others watch.

III. Thou Shalt Give Your Students a Reason to Read the Bible

Before ever asking students to read a Bible passage, let them know what information they're looking for. For example, before reading Luke 2:21–38, challenge students to find the two people who were waiting to meet baby Jesus and why. If they read the passage before the question, they'll always read the passage again after the question. Give the question first to communicate that the Bible is the source of answers. More examples: What does Moses' experience in Exodus 3:11–4:16 teach you about how to handle your fears? When is it right to limit your freedom for the sake of someone else's spiritual growth? If you know it is right, is it always OK to do? See what 1 Corinthians 8:1–13 says about this.

IV. Thou Shalt Insist That Your Students Base Their Answers on Scripture

When you ask a question or make an assignment, let your students know what passage holds the answers. Then insist that they quote from it at least once during the assignment. This helps students gain new Bible knowledge each session. Without it, students will use old knowledge or general principles such as "be loving." Questions like these ensure that the youth will consult Scripture:

- What did Jesus say about power based on Philippians 4:13?
- Write a new verse to a commercial tune that promotes spiritual gifts. Quote from Ephesians 4:11–16 at least three times in your commercial.
- Write a recipe for reconciliation based on Matthew 18:15–17. Choose two or more ingredients from the passage, and tell how to use them.

V. Thou Shalt Guide Your Students to Add a "Why?" or "How?"

Refuse to settle for the standard five church answers: (1) "Go to church," (2) "Read your Bible," (3) "Pray," (4) "Love one another," and (5) "Witness." Prod students to go deeper so they can discover not only what God wants them to do but how and why to do it. Move students to practical application with prompters like these:

- What sentence would you use in your prayer about that?
- What action would show you believe that?
- How have you seen this Bible principle happen at your school/home?
- Why is obeying God in this worth the effort?

When youth voice the reason for God's rule, they understand that rule and tend to obey it. When students can give an example of how to live a Bible truth, they live it. When students can describe their relationship with God, they grow closer to him.

VI. Thou Shalt Include a Rule That All Youth Participate

As youth participate in Bible study, they grow to believe they're a significant part of the class and, consequently, of God's kingdom. So prompt every student to talk, draw, write, and answer with a lighthearted, but firm, rule that everybody participate. This keeps some from looking like teacher's pet by volunteering and others from hesitating because it's uncool to answer. If students know they have to participate, they don't have to work up as much courage to do so. Because some students are natural talkers and some are naturally quiet, choose methods that guide all students to contribute equally, such as **Under Chair Questions** (see chapter 6). You'll find equalizing methods in chapters 6 (questions) and 8 (talk starters).

Perhaps even more important than the method you choose is your attitude toward each youth who contributes. Refuse the too tempting tendency to see some students as more spiritual than others. The ones who give spiritual-sounding answers may be the snakes in the church hallways. Instead of saying, "Be like Ben; he's such a good Christian!" say, "Be like Jesus." Then be just as excited about Elaine's answer as Ben's. Deliberately and openly treasure each student in your class by noticing the good God created in each. Ben answers lots of questions; Elaine welcomes people quietly but definitely; and Bill's obnoxious questions are on target more often than not—he may have the spiritual gift of prophecy.

VII. Thou Shalt Welcome Every Answer

It takes tremendous courage for most students to speak up in class. When they try, make them glad they did. Those who struggle in school will worry that they'll look dumb. The school-smart will worry that they don't have Bible knowledge. The talkative will assume they should talk. The quiet will assume someone else's answer is more valued. So deliberately value each contribution to communicate that everybody matters to God. For right answers, respond with: "Good job! You're right on target!" For partially right answers, try: "You're on the right track. What else does verse 23 say about that?" For totally off-the-wall answers, try something like, "I'm pleased that you spoke up. This is a hard question, and your answer is one many people give. How does verse 30 answer the question better?" For dangerously wrong answers, try something like, "I can't agree with your conclusion because the Bible says ___ and that conclusion would hurt people by ___. What other conclusion would be more true to life?"

Each time youth's answers are welcomed, they stay involved with the study. If their contributions are ignored, ridiculed, or rejected, youth will withdraw, learn less, and assume they're a failure at Christianity. Many stop coming. Don't underestimate the power of the way you welcome or unconsciously reject youth's answers. Just as important, classmates will imitate your cues on how they treat each other.

VIII. Thou Shalt Never Answer Thine Own Question

The one who talks is the one who learns. So silently count to ten after asking questions—fifty if you count fast. Resist the temptation to answer your own question if students take "too long." Because you have been thinking about the question since you prepared the lesson, the answer is on the tip of your tongue. But your students have just heard it—they need some time to think about it. If after twenty seconds no one answers, rephrase the question or give a more specific verse to look in. If you've asked a specific student, keep rephrasing until that original student answers. Don't let others jump in; the original student will miss the learning if others answer for her.

Continuously remind yourself that every time your students find a Bible answer, interpret a passage well, or make a wise point in class, they gain confidence in their own ability to read and understand and live the Bible for themselves. Answering your own questions, or letting other students answer for them, takes away this privilege. Let students discover and speak their own answers.

IX. Thou Shalt Affirm Ways Your Students Live Their Faith

Here's where the water hits the wheel. The true test of youth's Bible understanding is whether they live it day to day. So notice when they do this. Every time you notice and point out a way a student lives faith, you give him or her confidence to live it again. You show what spirituality really is. It's not talking with a holy sounding chant or going to church all the time. It's refusing to bite with your words, and deliberately treasuring the people around you. It's building your house on a rock and choosing to date people who bear rock-building fruits like joy, peace, kindness, and patience. It's resisting temptation, both the temptation to do wrong and the temptation to refuse right. It's recognizing that everything—even your attitude during a simple board game—is an opportunity to honor God.

Your attention reminds students that they really can live the Bible, that God really does equip them to manage the little parts of life. Comments like these point out faith actions:

- "I like the way you welcomed Meghan today. Way to be like Jesus!"
- "That answer is a new way to look at the passage! Brilliant."
- "Your encouraging smile helped me do the right thing. Thanks!"
- "Mr. Brown saw you and your friends after the game Saturday and has been bragging on the way you guys were having fun in such good ways. I'm really proud of your testimony for Christ. You show that Christians really do have more fun!"

X. Thou Shalt Love Your Students and Yourself

The greatest faith action is love. Because of that, and because students frequently equate your love for them with God's love, make it a point to speak to each student every time you are together. Give personalized attention like, "How did that conversation go that you were worried about?" or "How's the studying for exams coming?"

In addition, give each student one outside contact each month. Send postcards, E-mail, telephone or give a visit. Don't make youth miss a meeting before you'll contact them. Instead, care consistently. Cite in your notes something good they do in your Bible study. Let them know they are very important to God and to you. Keep a tally list to make certain you regularly contact each one.

Part of loving students is taking good care of yourself as a teacher. They will watch the way you treat yourself and the way you let others treat you. And from this living lesson students will learn from you how to love their neighbors as themselves. They will see that staying home with your ill child is just as holy as coming to the service. They will watch how to talk out disagreements calmly rather than hold grudges.

As you follow the above ten commandments, you may become frustrated, exhilarated, defeated, and triumphant all in the same day. These pains and pleasures of working with students become less painful and more pleasurable when you follow this advice:

Enjoy students. Treasure each one. See the good in them, and let them know what you see (Philem. 4–7). Guide them toward success with Scripture by insisting they keep their Bibles open, by starting with obvious questions and moving to harder ones, by welcoming every answer, and by regularly commenting on ways they live their faith well. You're pilgrims together in this journey toward Christlikeness.

Find at least one other teacher you can talk with about teaching youth. Youth work is both delightful and exasperating. You need someone with whom to share both. Another teacher can share your joy of seeing someone participate who felt shy before or of watching a student make a decision to follow Christ in a new area. Another teacher will understand your frustration when you prepare but forget your main point and share your broken heart when one student ridicules another. The two of you can remind each other that your work with students can change lives—both yours and the students with whom you work.

Learn along with your students. There's no need to return to an adult class to learn. Participate in learning projects with your students. Fill out and share the worksheets, make that confession, say that speech, grade yourself. Be excited about new discoveries. Share your struggles to love people (no names of course). Together understand difficult spiritual truths and apply them to life. Certainly you're the adult—don't try to be a peer—but you and your students are both members of Christ's body. Feel free to say, "I'm not sure," or "I'd better think about that one." All this teaches that Christianity is a journey, a pilgrimage, a never-ending adventure of new discoveries and steady growth toward Christlikeness.

Part 2

❦

Bible Study Methods

Chapter 4

❦

Bible Reading

Make Bible Reading Purposeful and Memorable

Rationale: Students must read the Bible to know what it says. But too often Bible reading becomes a dull, routine preliminary to the rest of the lesson. Students may barely attend to the passage. Then when you give the assignment or ask the question, they read the passage again. The first reading didn't even register. So why not let the Bible question or assignment be your students' motivation to read the Bible? Give the assignment or question first—your students will read the passage with purpose, seeking to find answers. And they'll be more likely to remember what they read.

Teaching Tip: Encourage students to bring their own Bibles by using them during every Bible study—they'll see no reason to bring their Bibles if they don't have to open them. As students use their own Bibles, they locate passages, mark them, personalize them, live them. Do provide department extras for those who forget, all the while encouraging students to bring their own and noticing when they do.

Teaching Tip: The worst Bible-reading method is one you use all the time. So find a new way to read Scripture every week. Pick drama for dramatic passages such as parables. Choose mystery questions for passages students may have read but need to go more deeply into. Match the method to the type of passage. The same goes for understanding and applying the Bible: vary your methods from week to week to invite students to eagerly seek what the Bible has in store for them that week.

Teaching Tip: If your curriculum includes printed Scripture, use it sparingly, such as when an activity requires all to have the same translation. When you do guide your students to read Scripture printed somewhere besides between two leather covers, remind them that Scripture is still the Word of God whether it is written in a book, on papyrus, on a scroll, or on the wall.

Bible as Script

Explain to your students that one of the best ways to read and understand the Bible is to reenact Bible events. Challenge each student to discover how a character acted and felt by stepping into that character's shoes. Use the Bible passage as your script. Assign each student a role from the passage, and guide them to act it out, reading directly from their own Bibles. Choose passages with both singular and crowd parts so everyone has a role—allow no spectators. Rather than use a narrator, instruct students to read their character's actions as well as words. Stand right in the middle of the action to direct it. Move students into position, point out who talks next, show them what actions to dramatize, and more. Throughout the drama, praise your students' good work, and stress that the Bible is full of real-life drama.

After the drama invite the student who played each role to be the authority on that character's role, commenting on what that character teaches and how to apply that truth to life. For example, the older son in the Luke 15 parable could explain why he hesitated to join in the celebration of his younger brother coming home and how to overcome similar hesitations today.

Adaptation: Allow students to play inanimate objects such as the tower in the parable of the tenants. Even the tower student who watches from his post is amazed to discover that the prophets and Jesus were treated so horribly.

Cued Reading

Guide your students to read a passage with cued comments. These one-word pauses or single-word questions challenge students to zero in on aspects of the passage they may not have noticed before. This method is especially effective in passages with big words or complex truths. It motivates students to find out what the confusing words mean and how to live them. Follow the reading with a **Word Study** (chapter 11) or another explanatory step. Here's how to do a cued reading:

1. Type a copy of your passage. Add cues in uppercase letters, enclosed in brackets.
2. Prepare cue cards to match the cues.
3. Enlist student cue card holders.
4. Seat cue card holders at the front of the group with a copy of the cued passage.
5. Instruct students to listen as you read the passage and to speak as the card holders prompt them.

This 2 Timothy 1:8–11 sample needs these cue cards: [HUH?] [OH!] [CHEER]

Here's how the typed copy would look:

> Do not be ashamed [HUH?] then, of witnessing for our Lord [OH!]; neither be ashamed of me, a prisoner for Christ's sake [HUH?]. Instead, take your part in suffering for the Good News, [HUH?] as God gives you strength for it. [OH!]

> He saved us and called us to be his own people [CHEER] not because of what we have done [OH!], but because of his own purpose and grace [CHEER].

> He gave us this grace [HUH?] by means of Christ Jesus before the beginning of time, but now it has been revealed to us [OH!] through the coming of our Savior, Christ Jesus [CHEER]. (Based on GNB.)

Detail Find

Challenge students to find and mark certain details in the passage. They must read the passage to find the details, and these details focus them on the truth you want to emphasize. For example:

- Circle every use of the word *all* in Deuteronomy 6:4–5. Which *all* would be easiest for you? Hardest for you? Invite students to share advice for loving God thoroughly.
- Underline every question in Genesis 3:1–13. How did Satan use his question? What was Satan working toward? How did God use his questions? What was God working toward? How did God's questions bring good and Satan's question bring destruction?
- Read Mark 3:13–19 for the names of Jesus' twelve disciples.

Fill in the Blanks

Print a copy of Scripture with key words replaced by blanks. Challenge students to race to fill in the blanks, stressing that they look in their Bibles for the answers. This encourages students to focus on key words. Follow this up with **Object Talk** (chapter 8), **Word Study** (chapter 11), or another method from chapters 6 through 10.

Variation: Let students write the passage for each other with blanks to fill in. They'll learn while they write and when they fill words back into others' writings.

Find the Change

Guide students to compare a change-filled copy of the passage to the real thing. As they find correct words, they notice the truth. Challenge students to find the changes in pairs: one student reads the Scripture passage while the other circles and corrects the changes in the bogus version. Then highlight meanings of the correct words.

To prepare this, type the Bible passage word for word. Enclose key words in parentheses. Add a changed word before the correct word. Print a copy so you'll have an answer sheet. Then delete the words in parentheses, and print copies for your students. This example from Romans 1:18–20 has the correct words in parentheses. Print without these.

Circle and correct every change. Find the changes by comparing this retelling to Romans 1:18–20:

> The love (wrath) of God is being revealed from heaven toward (against) all the godliness (godlessness) and righteousness (wickedness) of men who reveal (suppress) the truth by their righteousness (wickedness), since what may be known about God is hidden from (plain to) them, because God has made it plain to them. For since the creation of the world God's visible (invisible) qualities—his temporary (eternal) power and divine nature—have been gradually (clearly) seen, being misunderstood (understood) from what has been made, so that men have excuses (are without excuse).

Find the Verse

Write facts about a passage on individual cards. Challenge each student to take a card and find the verse in the passage that matches that fact. Repeat until all the facts have been taken. Because students have to read all the verses to find the answer, they repeatedly read them and better retain Bible facts.

Variation: Write the facts on a worksheet, and let students work in pairs to find verses for all the facts. Scramble the order for an added challenge.

Footprint Reading

Write each word of your passage on a separate footprint and display them in a path to your Bible study room. Enjoy watching students read the footprints as they step on each.

Adaptation: Enlist students to help you make the footprints. They'll learn as they write and as they watch others read.

Adaptation: For longer passages, put a phrase on each footprint.

Mark Your Bible

Guide students to read the passage and to mark it with symbols that encourage them to learn more. Show them how to write with pencil in their own Bibles or the one borrowed from your department. If they prefer not to write in their Bibles, show them how to slip a card under the page and write on the card. Use three or four symbols at most, and post the meaning of the symbols. Choose from samples like these:

- o: circle what you like
- ?: question what puzzles you
- X: what you need to remove from your life
- →: arrow actions you want to take
- __: underline actions you want to avoid
- =: equal commands you're already obeying in your life
- !: exclaim over what makes you glad about God

Let the marking lead students naturally into talking about the passage: Students can share what puzzles them and can invite others to suggest how they can understand that passage. They can share what they like and exclaim over to recognize that they can always understand parts of a passage. They can use the X, →, __ , and = markings to discuss how to apply the Bible to their lives.

Missing Words

Read the passage aloud with words left out, and prompt students to fill in the missing words. Choose to omit key words to help students focus on those words. Leave different words out each time. Then let each student take a turn reading the passage and choosing which words to leave out. They learn while they read, and they'll learn while they fill in words.

My Favorite Verse

Students like to be the authority. When you ask them what verse they like in a particular passage, they'll read the passage repeatedly until they find a favorite, even if they never had a favorite in that passage before.

Adaptation: When leading a topical study, ask youth their favorite verse on that topic. They'll dig until they find a verse that applies. This gets them reading their Bibles and makes them an authority in a specific Bible area. Let students use a concordance to find the verses, or limit the search area to a single passage (see **Concordance Study** in chapter 11).

My Name in the Bible

Read the passage with your students' names in place of *you* and other personal pronouns. Their ears will perk up, and they'll search the passage for promises and instructions addressed to them. For example: "God will meet all of *Judy's* needs according to his glorious riches in Christ Jesus" (Phil. 4:19). Reading with names communicates that the Bible is a personal communication from our specifically caring God.

Mystery Question

Give students a question for which they must search the Scripture to find the answer. Mystery questions let Bible reading become a search for God's answers and a listening for God's advice. These sample questions motivate meaningful Bible reading:

- Look for James's view of faith in James 2:14–26.
- Find the fears Moses had about becoming a leader in Exodus 3:7–4:13.
- As you read, find the character that is most like you and why.

Names on Back

To guide students to read the Bible passage repeatedly, select key words or phrases from your passage, write each on a different strip of paper, and tape a strip to the back of each student. Do not allow any student to read the word or phrase on his or her own back. Instead, challenge them to discover the word/phrase by reading the passage and asking "yes" or "no" questions of the other students who can read their backs. Insist that the students search the Bible passage for questions to ask about the word/phrase. Once they find their word or phrase, urge them to answer questions for others until all discover their word or phrase.

Transition into Bible understanding by instructing students to find details about their words or phrases in the Bible passage, and then tell the value of their word or phrase to the passage. Provide student books or other commentary to help in this reporting.

Adaptation: If you have fewer students than words, play twice or add a new word to students as they guess their first one. If you have more students than words, duplicate words.

Order the Events

Make a deck of cards with pictures (or names) of Bible events covering the Bible passage you are studying. Put one event on each card. Scramble the cards and challenge students to read the passage so they can put the events in order. Race between teams to make this even more inviting.

Adaptation: Prepare a set of scrambled cards for every trio of students. The fewer the students on a team, the more each member is involved.

Adaptation: Let pairs of students prepare a set of events for the other teams. They learn twice: once while writing the Bible events in order, and once when sorting the scrambled events of the other teams.

Adaptation: Invite your more artistic students to draw the events ahead of time. Then photocopy a set for each group. These artists will learn both when drawing and when putting the events in order.

Out-of-Place Posters

Display a copy of the key Bible passage on a floor poster, ceiling poster, doorway cover, or other out-of-the-way place. An unusual location attracts students' attention and motivates them to read it. Increase interest by encoding the passage or presenting it in rebus form (words into pictures).

Read with Tools

When students encounter a confusing portion in their Bibles, they frequently quit reading. Prevent this tragedy by showing students how to use Bible study tools to dig out the answers they seek. Bring in a concordance, a Bible dictionary, and a Bible commentary. Let your students leaf through them. Show your students how they work. Help them remember which book is which with a matching game: Write a set of matching cards, one with the name of the tool and one with the description of the tool. Display these face down, and challenge students to take turns choosing two cards. If one card defines the other, they keep the cards; if not, they turn the cards back over. After all cards are matched, invite students to give 10-second testimonies of times they could use each tool. Sample cards:

Tool Name
- Concordance
- Bible Dictionary
- Commentary

Tool Description
- A listing of Bible words in alphabetical order with verses that use the word. This tool is handy for finding the verse you can't remember or for finding a series of verses on a Bible word.
- This tool defines words used in the Bible. It may have simple one-line definitions or multiple-page explanations. One especially geared for students is the *Holman Student Bible Dictionary*.
- This tool contains one or more Bible student's insights into the meaning of Bible passages. It's like sitting down to talk with another Christian who can help you understand a Bible passage. Your Sunday school book is an example of this.

Walk and Read

Create Bible reading posters by folding paper in half, writing a question about the passage inside each poster, including the verse in the Bible where the answer is found, numbering the poster on the outside, and posting the posters in order around the room. As students enter the room, point out the flip posters and challenge students to find facts about the passage by answering the question inside each one. Students will have to read the Bible passage to find each answer. And the walking makes the reading more intriguing.

Provide paper to write answers. Then debrief by giving each student one flip poster and letting him be the authority on that question. Privately let them tell you their answer before reporting it to the group. Gently show them the verse in which to find any answers they have not yet found.

Variation: Post the posters in scrambled order so students have to seek out the next one.

This sample guides students to study 1 Corinthians 15. Do not print the answers, which are in italics.
- Flip Poster 1: Read 1 Corinthians 15:1–4 for the three main facts of the gospel. *(1-Christ died for our sins; 2-Christ was buried; 3-Christ raised on the third day)*
- Flip Poster 2: Read 1 Corinthians 15:5–8 to name six people or groups of people Jesus appeared to after his resurrection. *(1-Peter; 2-the Twelve; 3-More than five hundred brothers; 4-James; 5-all the apostles; 6-Paul)*
- Flip Poster 3: Read 1 Corinthians 15:9–11 to discover what Paul called himself. *(the least of the apostles)*

- Flip Poster 4: Read 1 Corinthians 15:12–13 to discover who has not been raised if there is no resurrection. *(Jesus Christ)*
- Flip Poster 5: Read 1 Corinthians 15:14–19 for five sad results if Christ has not been raised. *(1-our preaching is useless; 2-so is your faith; 3-we are found to be false witnesses; 4-those who are dead in Christ are lost; 5-we have hope only in this life).*
- Flip Poster 6: Read 1 Corinthians 15:20–22 to discover in whom we all die and in whom we all can be resurrected. *(die in Adam; will be made alive in Christ)*
- Flip Poster 7: Read 1 Corinthians 15:23–28 to find out at least three things that will happen when Jesus comes back. *(those who belong to him will be made alive; the end will come; he will put enemies under his feet; God will be all in all)*

Who Am I?

Guide students to discover characteristics and actions of important Bible characters (or things) by using "Who am I?" cards. Write each description, making certain that the answers are directly in the Bible passage and require no extra information. Fan them in your hands and invite each student to take one and discover its identity in the Bible passage you provide. This can be especially effective with familiar passages — students are pleasantly surprised to discover something new.

Adaptation: Guide students to write their own "Who am I?" cards and then exchange. Provide a list of people and objects from the passage about which to write cards.

Adaptation: Guide students to write cards about themselves as a get-to-know-you activity or as an expression of their commitment to Christ.

Word Search Plus

As students arrive, give them a word search puzzle containing key words from the day's passage. Instead of referring to a list of words to find, students must search the Bible passage for key words. This encourages new study because students read the passage repeatedly to complete this assignment.

A basic word search consists of rows of letters, some of which spell words. Create word searches by selecting key words from the passage you are studying. Write these on graph paper (or your computer) vertically, horizontally, and diagonally. Write some of the words backwards. Fill in the blank squares with random consonants (no vowels to keep from spelling words accidentally). Duplicate one copy for each student.

To enhance a word search *while* the students are seeking the words, include these activities.

- *Where?* Each time students find a word in the word search puzzle, direct them to write the verse in which the word is used.
- *How Many?* Tell students how many words to find. Encourage them to check off the words in their Bibles as they find them.
- *How long?* Direct students to race against the clock to find the words.
- *Race.* Divide into pairs and motivate students to compete against one another. Good-natured competition is almost always a good motivator for Bible reading.

Enhance a word search *after* students have completed it:

- *Summary sentence.* Instruct students to summarize the passage in one sentence, using as many of the word search words as they can without repeating the Bible verses themselves.
- *My favorite word.* Invite each student to choose a word and tell what it teaches them about God or the specific Bible concept the group is studying.
- *My favorite phrase.* Invite each student to read a favorite verse or verse portion that uses one of the words and tell why she likes it.

Plus . . .

Try these other options for reading your Bible passage:

- Print the passage with no spaces. Students divide the words correctly, comparing to their Bibles to verify. This activity is called **Squashed Together Letters** in chapter 5.
- Play **Letter Board, Word That Definition,** or any Bible learning game from chapter 5. These require repeated reading so that by the time the game is over, students have digested the passage.
- Read the passage in unison several times, each time more quickly than before.
- Read responsively.
- Do a conversational reading, with the students pretending to be Bible characters.
- Find what the passage teaches about God's character or expectations.
- Invite students to look for the phrase in an assigned passage that most specifically speaks to their lives at this time.

Chapter 5

🎀

Learning Games

*Games can attract and focus
attention on the Bible.*

Rationale: Bible teaching does not have to be separate from the fun. In fact, serious fun is one of the best ways to honor God. When you use a Bible learning game, you guide youth to learn Bible facts in meaningful and lasting ways. Because they want to do well, they learn Bible facts and grow ready to understand those facts in the next steps. Always play games with an open Bible and from a single passage, the one for that Bible study. When used well, games become meaningful ways to learn for several reasons:

Youth want to succeed in front of their peers. In games like **Bible Tic-Tac-Toe**, no one has to miss a question for the game to work. All they have to do is keep reading the Bible passage and they will find the answer. Success with the Bible, not winning or losing, is the goal of any Bible learning game. Choose games in which looking in the Bible becomes the key to the win.

Youth want to look spiritually smart. Well-designed learning games give students the opportunity to shine. A game gives youth less "school fear" than a discussion or worksheet. When the answers come directly from the Bible, even new-to-church youth can find them. They gain confidence in their ability to answer and understand Bible questions.

Moving encourages attention. If the body is moving, the brain can't go to sleep. And youth's natural interest in games focuses them on the key to a win—the Bible passage. Learning games invite active participation from the entire group.

Youth don't realize they're learning. Those who believe they can't learn are able to relax and learn more effectively with learning games. Those who think they already know it all usually learn something new.

Success with the Bible in class motivates use of the Bible at home. When students successfully find answers in their Bibles during a game, they grow the habit of looking to God's Word for answers at home.

Teaching Tip: Encourage students to keep their Bibles open at all times during learning games. If they don't bring their own Bible, give them one. The goal of learning games is to learn new Bible facts, not to drum up old knowledge.

Teaching Tip: Avoid Bible games that pull questions from the entire Bible or from several passages at once. Even the best Bible students have difficulty succeeding at these. Focus on one or two passages so players can learn the passage(s) thoroughly.

Teaching Tip: Let youth's natural drive toward competition become a motivation to pay attention to Scripture, not a tool for putting down losers. In the best learning games, extra points are given for encouraging other teams, and every team wins at least one round.

Teaching Tip: Ways to compete include person vs. person, person vs. clock, team vs. team, and team vs. clock.

Teaching Tip: Draw game questions from questions in your curriculum, or make up your own questions. Just make certain the questions come directly from the Bible passage. Opinions and interpretations are for other Bible study methods.

Teaching Tip: Make an answer key for yourself. Write the question, followed by the verse reference, followed by the answer. In the excitement of leading the game you may find it hard to recall answers.

Teaching Tip: To avoid complaints of favoritism in the distribution of questions, let players request a question by number without seeing the list.

Teaching Tip: Games are usually best as the first step because they lay the groundwork for moving into deeper study.

Teaching Tip: Most games in this chapter include these elements:

- *Process of Play*: A step by step guide to leading the game.
- *Rules:* Use these to explain the game to students. Consider posting them.
- *Follow-up*: Ideas for making the most of the game's teaching potential.
- *Adaptations*: To use if time, players, or space is short.

Bible Concentration

The goal of concentration games is to turn over identical cards from a set of face-down cards. Adapt this to Bible learning by matching not identical cards, but cards that complete one another. Here are some examples of types of completions:

- Half a Bible phrase on one card and the other half of the Bible phrase on the other card. Put the Bible reference on the second half only.
- A Bible person's name on one card and something that person did or said on the other card. Put the Bible reference on the did/said card only.
- A Bible person's name on one card and a description of that person on the other. Put the Bible reference on the description card only.
- A Bible term on one card and a definition on the other. Put the page from the Bible dictionary on the definition card only.

A study of the last week of Jesus' life might use matches from Mark 14–16. Sample matches:

PETER   *said he would never deny Jesus but denied him three times (Mark 14:72)*

SOLDIERS   *mocked Jesus with a purple robe and a crown of thorns (Mark 15:16–20)*

Process of Play

1. Create the game by writing cards that complete one another. For the best learning, let students find and write the matches. Give each youth two cards and a verse on which you want them to write a match.
2. Shuffle the cards, turn them over, and number them. Display them in rows (eight, twelve, sixteen, or twenty-four cards make the rows even).
3. Prepare one game for every two to six students. Explain the rules.
4. Display the game, number side up, and challenge students to take turns flipping over two cards at a time. If the cards match, they keep them. If not, they flip them back over. Direct students to always verify their answers in their Bibles.

Rules

1. Turn over two cards at a time. If they match, keep them. If not, turn them back over. Verify your matches with the Bible references.
2. Even if you make a correct match, it is still the next person's turn. This gives everyone more chances.
3. Watch each other's pairs so you can remember where the cards lie. This allows you to make future matches.

Follow-up

Distribute the matches evenly. Invite each student to tell about the match(es) in his hand, using their Bibles and student-book commentary. Supplement from your teacher's book or commentary.

Adaptations

- Enlist an artistic youth to draw a rebus to place under the concentration game. A rebus is a combination of words and pictures that states the theme or focal verse of your Bible study (see chapter 13). Challenge students to solve the rebus as they make matches.
- Guide each pair of students to make concentration games for the other pairs. They learn twice: once creating the game and once playing.

Bible Jeopardy

This Bible learning game gives the answers and invites students to ask the questions. It works well with a detailed passage, when studying a large amount of text, or when reviewing several sessions.

Process of Play

1. Choose five categories. Your five categories might include one category for each session of a five-session study, one for each section of a student book, or one for each of five parts of a long passage.
2. Write twenty-five jeopardy answers, five each in the five categories, with matching questions. Writing jeopardy answers can be more tricky than it sounds because some answers match several questions (such as the answer "Jesus"). To keep this from happening, write your questions first and then change to answer form. For example, when you want your students to know from Genesis 9:3, "What could Noah eat that he could not eat before?" your answer becomes, "What Noah could eat that he could not eat before," not "meat." Here are more examples:

What blessing did God give Noah and his sons?	*Becomes*	The blessing God gave Noah and his sons (Gen. 9:9–11).	*and the question is:* What is "I now establish my covenant with you and with your descendants after you . . . Never again will all life be cut off by the waters of a flood; never again will there be a flood to destroy the earth"?
What does the rainbow stand for?	*Becomes*	The meaning of the rainbow (9:13).	*and the question is:* What is the sign of God's covenant never to flood the earth again?

3. Arrange the answers in order of difficulty within each category, the easiest worth ten points and the hardest worth fifty points.
4. Set up the game up one of these ways:
   • Write each answer on a page and cover it with a page declaring its point value. Write the correct question on the back of its answer page. Tape these to the wall, like the game show, in category rows. When students choose a point value, lift the point page to reveal the answer to be questioned.
   • Write each answer on paper and place it in an envelope marked with the point value. Make an answer key of correct questions. Youth open the envelope to reveal the answer. Reuse these envelopes for future games.
   • Write the answers on a single piece of white paper in rows. Make an overhead cell of this paper. Tape a square over each answer. Make an answer key with the correct questions and verse references. Project the "board" on the wall. Lift the papers to reveal the answers.
5. Explain the rules below.
6. If your group is small, challenge the students to play individually. If your group is large, play in teams, encouraging teams to consult one another before giving answers. See chapter 16 for suggestions for forming teams.
7. Play and enjoy, encouraging students to keep their Bibles open to today's passage to find the questions.

Rules

1. The person with the birthday closest to today chooses the first category and point value.
2. Once the answer is read, the first person to stand questions the answer. Because you lose points for incorrect questions, think and consult before standing. Because you are racing against others, stand as soon as you think you know.
3. The last correct questioner chooses the next category and point value.
4. Correct questioners earn the points for that answer. Incorrect questioners lose the points for that answer.
5. Keep your Bibles open to the passage at all times. To be correct, you must name the verse where you got the answer.

Follow-up

- Comment on answers as they are questioned. In this way the game becomes the vehicle for Bible understanding. You teach the Bible lesson as youth learn the facts.
- Affirm teamwork. Give extra points for encouraging both their own team and the other teams. Point out how students help each another find questions.
- Pay positive attention to students who try, even if they're unsuccessful.

Adaptations

- Let students create their own answers week by week. Then incorporate these into a review jeopardy game. Remind students to write the answer on a page and the matching question on the back of that page with the Bible reference. You pick point values. Students will have the easiest time with the answers they wrote, but that's a bonus for being there weekly.
- To keep students focused on the passage you're studying, direct them to keep their Bibles open to the passage and put their finger on the verse that gives the question. Give credit only if they can name the verse.
- Feel free to adapt the number of categories to four or six, three or seven.

Bible Tic-Tac-Toe

To review units of study or to do detail study on a specific passage, play **Bible Tic-Tac-Toe** with students as the markers. It is a great fact-focus procedure:

Process of Play

1. Arrange the chairs in three rows of three chairs, like a tic-tac-toe board. Arrange remaining chairs in two groups, one group on each side, facing the human-size board:

X	⊢ ⊢ ⊢	0
players	⊢ ⊢ ⊢	players
here	⊢ ⊢ ⊢	here

2. Get questions from your curriculum or by writing them yourself. Choose questions that can be answered directly from the Bible passage.

You'll need at least nine questions for each round of play. Number the questions and write the verse reference and answer after each.

3. Cut paper X's and O's from half sheets of paper. Prepare loops made of tape to attach the X's and O's to the students.

4. Divide your group into two teams using a suggestion in chapter 16. Seat teams on opposite sides of the tic-tac-toe "board." Give one team paper X's and the other team O's. Provide masking tape to attach the X/O's like name tags. Insist that all students wear them. Explain that they are the markers for the tic-tac-toe board.

5. Explain and play by the rules (below).

6. Challenge each team to seat three correct answerers in a row. The only coaching they can give is to choose the chair where the teammate sits. Then they must be quiet and let the teammate find the answer in the Bible.

7. Stress that the game is open Bible—all answers come directly from the Bible passage, and students must look in their Bibles for the answers. Post the Bible verses for easy reference.

8. Call for an X to sit in a chair on the tic-tac-toe board and answer the question they choose. (If X is incorrect he must return to his team.) Repeat for O. Continue alternating until one team seats three students in a row. If they form a cat's-eye, award points to both teams and begin again. Award extra points for encouraging the other team.

Rules

1. An X brings his Bible to the tic-tac-toe board and sits in the chair his team chooses. Because some questions are harder than others, X requests a Bible question by number.

2. The team member must answer with no help from his team but with lots of help from his Bible. If correct, X stays in the chair. If not, X returns.

3. The O's must pay close attention while X is in the chair. If X misses, the O's may consult among themselves and send a member to answer that same question. If O misses, the X's may consult and send a member to answer the same question.

4. No team member may play a second time before all play once.

5. The decision of the judge is final.

6. Particularly encouraging words, especially for the opposing team, may be rewarded with extra points.

Follow-up

- As each question is answered, briefly comment on that section of the Bible passage. Let commentary flow naturally from the game process. For example, when you ask "What did God say about Jesus when he was baptized?" and *X* answers, "'This is my Son, whom I love; with him I am well pleased,'" explain that these words show that Jesus is God's Son and that Jesus' baptism marked the formal beginning of his ministry on earth.
- Following the game, congratulate your students' brilliant performance and note that during this game they studied the Bible. Stress that just as they found the game answers by looking in their Bibles, they can look in their Bibles to find the answers to the game of life.

Adaptations

- If your room is too small to set up three rows of chairs, "draw" a tic-tac-toe board with masking tape on the floor. Students can stand on the squares.
- If your room is too small for floor squares, display a tic-tac-toe board on the table or wall and let students place their *X*'s and *O*'s.
- This game is best with groups of ten to twenty students but can be played with as few as two. With smaller groups, students leave "*X/O*" in the chair.
- If someone misses, state that she had hard question. Teens find it easier to accept missing a hard question than an easier one. Praise all efforts. Impose no time limit so students can search the passage at their pace.

Bible Trivia

In this room-size trivia game, questions come from the Bible passage you are studying. Correct answers are rewarded with triangles in six colors. The first team to collect all six triangles wins. After students answer a question they roll a colored die to tell what triangle their team earns. If they already have a triangle in that color, they don't win another. The presence of the die and the work for six triangles motivates students to pay attention and answer questions. As with all learning games, write your questions directly from Scripture and instruct your students to keep their Bibles open and take their answers directly from Scripture. Post the passage you are studying.

Process of Play

1. Write a set of numbered questions that cover your passage.
2. Cover a standard die with six construction paper squares. Rubber cement holds them on nicely and then allows them to be removed later.
3. Cut six triangles for each team from the six colors on your die.
4. Divide students into teams of about four. Seat the teams opposite each other in the shape the number of teams form: three teams in a triangle, four teams in a square, five teams in a pentagon, and so on.
5. Explain and play by the rules (below).

Rules

1. The first team requests a question by number and confers with all team members before answering. There is no time limit, but the first answer is the only answer allowed. Be certain each answer comes directly from the Bible passage and is not a guess.
2. If correct, the team rolls the die and receives a triangle in the color that comes up. Display the triangles on the floor in front of the team. If a team rolls a color it already has, it wins no triangle.
3. Teams take turns answering and rolling until one team has triangles in all six colors.
4. Every student must have a turn before any teammate takes a second.
5. The decision of the judge is final. If a player's translation varies in wording, the player's translation will be the correct one.

Follow-up

Comment on questions as they are answered so the game becomes the vehicle for Bible study. After the game, quiz youth briefly to demonstrate how much they have learned about the passage.

Adaptations

- Let the students write the trivia questions, each assigned to a different portion of the Scripture you are studying. Then let the game close the session. The teams who wrote the questions get to ask the others.
- Use the game to study commentary text from your student book or theme materials. It works well with large bodies of material.
- Prepare the questions in categories, and let the students roll the die to choose a category. If they answer correctly, they win a triangle in that color. Use the categorized version when studying several passages,

when studying a long passage with many details, or when reviewing several weeks of study.

- Make the questions extremely trivial but obvious in the passage to get students looking in their Bibles. Remind them that no bit of Bible information is trivial, and the answers are always in the Bible. Always play open Bible.
- Firmly avoid trivia games that focus on the whole Bible. Instead use questions from passages you're currently studying or have recently studied.

Category Call-out

Popularized as Scattergories, this game challenges students to call out items that match a Bible category. Particularly good for application, this listing activity helps students discover that God's Word applies to all situations. It can also be used to introduce a passage by stimulating interest in the many situations answered by the passage.

Process of Play

1. Form teams of two to six students using one of the team-forming methods in chapter 16.
2. Give each team a three-by-five-inch card and a pencil. Direct them to number the card one through six.
3. Assign a letter by rolling a letter cube or calling on a youth to name the middle letter of his or her middle name.
4. Name a category based on your passage, and direct students to write six things that both fit that category and begin with the assigned letter. Sample categories:
- Circumstances that tempt Christian teenagers
- Ways to resist those temptations
- How to do good on purpose so temptation has less power
- Reasons we're glad we follow Jesus
5. Call for each team to name one item on its list of six. If no one else has listed that item, they circle it. If anyone else has it, *all* teams cross it off. The point is to look for unique answers.
6. Repeat for another category related to your theme.

Rules

1. Your goal is to list six items that both begin with that round's letter and match that round's category.

2. Work as a team.

3. Seek answers that you think no other team will have, but write down every answer you think of. Narrow down answers later if you have time.

Follow-up

- Highlight that the game is a fun way to list things we go through and to discover the many ways God can help. Stress that though all answers are valid, the unique ones help us see something we might not have otherwise seen.

- Invite each youth to choose one listing and say two sentences about it. For a particular temptation, they could tell two ways God could help us resist it.

Adaptations

- After a round or two, let students choose the categories, drawing from the Bible passage you're studying.

- Always play with a single theme or Bible passage rather than with the whole Bible. Why? The goal of a Bible learning game is to thoroughly digest that theme or passage, not to remember past knowledge. In addition, even the most experienced Bible scholar can feel ignorant during whole-Bible games.

Cootie Catcher

Remember those fun paper folds with eight flaps to lift that we created in elementary school? We called them "cootie catchers." All youth except seventh graders will delight in making them again—seventh graders are trying to leave childhood, but others are glad to return to it for a season.

Guide students to make cootie catchers when you have eight facts, eight people, or eight quotes you want them to discover. When studying Luke 2 during the Christmas season, you might challenge your students to find eight characters and what they did. On each first flap they would write the name of the person and on the inside flap what that character did or said. Then on the outside four wings, they would compose a four-word phrase to summarize the actions or words of the eight, such as "Those who welcomed God." Insist that students quote directly from Scripture so they learn the passage inside and out.

Process of Play

1. Guide each student to create from plain white paper a cootie catcher like in elementary school. Most will remember just how to make them, but these steps can guide the process:

a. First fold one corner of 8 1/2-by-11-inch paper to the other side and cut off the leftover strip to form a folded square. Open the square back up and fold it to the other corner. Open it.

b. Fold each corner of this square to the center and crease the folded edges.

c. Fold over each corner of this smaller square to the center on the other side. Crease the folded edges.

d. Fold the puzzle in half, making a rectangle.

e. Unfold the rectangle and fold in half again making another rectangle, except in the opposite direction of the first. Open back up.

f. Put four fingers, two from each hand, in the open flaps on the underside and pinch inward.

2. Guide students to look in your passage for eight characters and write those names on the eight flaps inside the cootie catcher (Samples for Luke 2 include: Caesar Augustus, Quirinius, Joseph, Mary, Baby Jesus, Shepherds, angels/heavenly host, Simeon, Holy Spirit, Anna, temple teachers).

3. On the flap under each name, guide students to write what that character did or said, quoting exactly from the Bible. For example, Simeon "took him [Jesus] in his arms and praised God" (Luke 2:28).

4. After completing the eight sections, both outside and inside, return to the outside four sections. Write one word per section using the words "Those who welcomed God" or another four-word phrase that matches the passage you're studying.

5. Now that the cootie catchers are complete, guide students to work in pairs to take turns flipping their cootie catchers, spelling the outside words, then a name of one person on the inside, and then opening the flap of the one they pick to find out what they did or said.

Rules

1. Using plain white paper, create a cootie catcher that teaches about eight people in Luke 2, as guided by your teacher.

2. Remember to quote directly from Scripture.

3. Invite a partner to pick an outside word: "Those," "who," "welcomed," or "God." Spell it, opening one way for one letter, the other way for the next. When you finish, pick a flap from the four open ones. Spell it, opening one way or the other for each letter. Then pick a flap from the four open ones and look underneath to see what that person did or said.

Follow-up

- Explain that just as moving the puzzle helped us discover Bible facts, letting God move our lives helps us discover the good he has in mind for us.
- Highlight that manipulating the puzzle guided students to memorize the role eight characters played in the coming of Jesus Christ. Ask each student which character, besides Jesus, they would most want to know and why. Prompt each to choose a different character.

Adaptations

- Adapt the words and themes for whichever Bible passage you are studying.
- If your group does not divide evenly into pairs to flip the cootie catchers, form trios or pair up with a student yourself.
- Remember to stay in a single passage for deeper learning.

Detailed Descriptions

In this game, popularized as Balderdash, students write three descriptions for a Bible word, only one of which is accurate. The goal is to make the impostors so believable that listeners have a hard time identifying them. The advantage is that students learn to distinguish truth from falsehood, even when wrong sounds right. They also learn the meanings of tough Bible terms. Students use their Bibles to write the true descriptions, which enhances the pattern of letting the Bible guide their understanding.

Process of Play

1. Choose a passage with lots of big words. Ephesians 2 is an example. It includes *transgressions, sins, spirit, sinful nature, wrath, love, mercy, grace, saved, Christ, faith, workmanship,* and much more.
2. Invite each student to choose a different word and to use a Bible and Bible dictionary to write one authentic description and two impostors. Suggest they quote part of the verse in which they find the word. They may want to supplement with **Concordance Study** (see chapter 11).
3. Call for students to read the word and the three descriptions numbered one, two, and three. The rest of the students are to write down the number of the definition they think is correct, based on the passage.
4. Prompt the students to call out the correct answer. Give points for every stump to the reader; give points for every correct identification to the listener.

Rules

1. Choose one word from the Bible passage.
2. Use your Bible, a Bible dictionary, and a concordance to write an accurate description or definition of that word.
3. Write two descriptions that sound right but aren't. Try to stump your classmates with little deviations from truth.

Follow-up

- Discuss why little deviations are some of the most dangerous and how we can let the Bible show us what is really true.
- Highlight that just because something sounds right doesn't mean it is right. Invite students to tell ways they can distinguish Bible truth from imitations.

Adaptations

- Use the two wrong/one right description approach when studying cults, new age, or other counterfeit religions. Include the cults' descriptions for God, Jesus, and more, paired with the Bible's descriptions. Award points for the students who are able to identify the truth. Stress that many religious groups use spiritual words, but they don't define the words correctly.
- Consider writing the trio of descriptions yourself to highlight some commonly used deceptions.

Fact Match

Write the first half of a Bible fact on one card and the second half on a second card. Include the Bible reference on the second card only. Shuffle all the cards and challenge students to match them correctly. This can be done several ways:

- *Human Match:* Give each youth a card and challenge them to find the person who holds the card that matches theirs. They verify their matches in the Bible.
- *Match Race:* Make two sets of cards and give one set each to two teams. Challenge each team to race to match the cards before the other team does. Encourage them to keep their eyes on their Bible passage as they match.
- *Concentration:* Shuffle the cards and display them face down. Guide youth to take turns turning over two cards. If they match, keep them. If not, turn them back over.

- *Match in My Hand:* Hold the first half of each match in your hand. Display the second halves randomly on the floor or table. Hold one up and challenge youth to find its match.
- *Here's My Card:* Let students draw an unseen card from your hand and match it to a card on the floor.

Follow-up

Each time the students make a match, invite them to tell why that fact is important to the Bible event, how it influences their life, or what they like about it. Refer them to the Bible passage and to your student-book commentary.

Father, May I?

Adapt the childhood game "Mother, May I?" to guide youth to talk about why they want to obey God's guidelines. The one giving permission must quote the verse that gives permission and tell a reason the Father wants us to do that. Rotate permission givers so all students have experience finding the verses and giving reasons. Once again, stick to a single Bible passage to thoroughly digest it.

Guess My List

Popularized as Outburst, the object of this Bible study game is to guess the items on a list within a specific category. The best way to play during Bible study is to assign a category, let teams of students make the lists from the Bible passage, and then guess each other's lists. While studying Genesis, students might list six items God created (*light, day, night . . .*), or six actions/ quotes from Adam and Eve. Play open Bible and with a time limit. This provides double learning, once while listing the items, and once while guessing the items.

Process of Play

1. Form teams of two to four students according to a team-forming method in chapter 16.
2. Assign each team a portion of the Bible passage you're studying. It's OK to give all teams the same passage or assignment. Each list will be slightly different, and it will help students repeat the learning, a powerful retention process.

3. Direct each team to write down ten items from the Bible passage that match the assignment you give. Be certain there are at least ten of those in that passage.
4. Call for teams to take turns rapidly guessing each other's lists.

Rules

1. Keep your Bible open. The object is to find the items in today's Bible passage and call them out, not to recall randomly what you've learned in the past.
2. Work for speed as well as accuracy.
3. Let your whole team call out answers at once.
4. Have at least two listeners to make sure you miss no one's contribution.

Follow-up

- Highlight that listing items from a Bible passage helps us search for details. Then guessing each other's lists helps us remember those details.
- Transition to an application of the Bible lists with a talking method from chapter 8, or a paper method from chapter 7.

Adaptations

- If there are only six items in the Bible passage, reduce to four of the items to list.
- For lists you want everyone to remember (such as the Ten Command-ments, or the nine Beatitudes), make the lists yourself. Then prompt youth to name them during class.

Letter Board

Popularized as Boggle, this game challenges students to circle all the words they can find in a block of letters. To make it good Bible study, create the letter board with four or five phrases from the Bible passage you are studying that day. In the process of the game, students will memorize that part of the Bible passage. The competition encourages involvement, and the Bible text shows students how to honor God. **Letter Board** works well as an arrival activity because early arrivers get the most words and thus receive positive attention for arriving on time.

Process of Play

1. Choose the phrases you want to stress from the day's Bible passage.

2. Type your phrases in all caps, one phrase to a line, with no spaces between words or between lines. Add these directions at the top: *Circle all the words you can find in this block of letters. Words can be vertical, horizontal, diagonal, backward, forward, or a combination of directions. You can count plural words twice (once in singular, once in plural) and words within words (example "Jesus" also contains "us"). Keep a tally of all the words you circle.*

3. Duplicate the letter boards, one for every pair of students. Explain and play by the following rules.

A sample letter board for Isaiah 9:6:

Rules

1. Your job is to circle and tally all the words you can find. Work closely with your partner.
2. Words you circle must be authentic. Proper names count.

Follow-up

- Challenge volunteers to repeat the game's four phrases without looking. The game process will have helped them memorize at least part of the phrases.
- Because students will complain if you don't score, call for each pair to count their words. Award the winning one with generous applause.

Adaptations

- Use phrases that relate to your theme such as in this example on forgiveness:

```
F O R G I V E N E S S H E A L S
R E L A T I O N S H I P S
Y O U D O N T H A V E T O F O R G E T T O F O R G I V E
B E I N G F O R G I V E N M A K E S
F O R G I V I N G E A S I E R
F O R G I V I N G H E A L S Y O U A N D
T H E O N E Y O U F O R G I V E
```

- Allow words made of any adjacent letters, even if the letters are not in a straight line. Examples: *font* and *hive* in the sample above.
- Guide students to create a letter board by writing the main truth of the lesson weekly. The truths become the letter board that you use for review.

Name the Word

This adaptation of the TV game *Password* is quick to prepare and easy to use. It results in memorizing a series of Bible words. It can be used to study key words in a passage or a series of theme words. Playing **Name the Word** with key words from a single passage motivates students to read the passage repeatedly and thus better understand and remember it. Playing with theme words is harder because youth must depend on several passages at once. Its value is pulling together a major Bible theme. Post the verses to make the game less frustrating.

Process of Play

1. Choose one passage and select the key words (or passwords) from it. Passwords from 1 Timothy 4:12 include *young, example, believers, speech, life, love, faith, purity.*

   If playing the theme version, choose a theme such as Names for Jesus (*Son of Man, Son of God, The Way, The Truth, The Life, The Door, Messiah, The Good Shepherd, The Gate.*) Other themes include: Characters in the Exodus, Books of the Bible. Use a topical Bible to find passages on your theme.

2. Prepare a set of password cards by writing each word on a separate card. Thicker cards keep youth from reading through the back.

3. Prepare one set of cards for every five youth expected. Four youth play the game and one serves as clue-giver/scorekeeper.

4. Overview the rules. Set up four facing chairs for each game. Partners face partners and sit next to opponents. In this illustration, b and B are partners, D and d are partners:

   B b
   D d

5. The clue-giver/scorekeeper (you, if your class is small) shows the first password to one side (capital letters in the illustration). B gives the first clue to his partner b. Clues are one-word hints that make the partner say the password. Possible clues for YOUNG might be "old" or "age."

6. If b answers correctly, the B's earn ten points. If not, D gives a one-word clue to d. If B said "old," D might mistakenly say "new." But then "teenager" would confirm that the word is "young." Clues build to make the password more obvious. If d is correct, the D's get nine points.
7. Alternate clue-giving until one is correct, or point value is zero.
8. In the next round, show the password to the other side (lowercase letters in illustration). Let *d* give the first clue so the *D*'s have a chance to make ten points. Alternate until all words are guessed or time expires.

Rules

1. Your job is to work with your partner to guess the passwords.
2. When you give a clue, use only one word and no part of the password. Use no gestures.
3. First guesses are final, even if they are a mistake. Think before speaking.
4. Alternate being first clue-giver and first guesser.
5. Listen to the clues of your opponent so your clues build on theirs.

Follow-up

- While playing, briefly discuss each word as it is guessed. If you are studying names of Christ you might ask: "How is Jesus like a *gate* in your life?" or "How does this name for Christ affect the way you relate to him?"
- After the game discuss in more detail questions that show how the words relate to each other. After guessing words on 1 Timothy 4:12, you might ask: "In what five areas can you be an example? How does each show your belief in God?"
- Invite volunteers to recite the verse you have studied by using the passwords as clues.

Adaptations

- This game can get confusing if students have several Bible translations. Accept as correct the answer that comes from the translation in the youth's lap. For example in 1 Timothy 4:12, "conduct" in the New American Standard Bible means the same as "life" in the New International Version.
- Guide students to make their own password cards for double learning—once while seeking the words and once while learning them during the game.

- If you have six students, play with three rows instead of two.
- If adults are available, let them serve as clue-givers/scorekeepers.

Newly Christian Game

Adapt the couples-ask-questions-to/about-each-other format of *The New-lywed Game* to Bible study with **The Newly Christian Game**. Rather than enlist pairs and put them in front of the group, pair every youth with another youth. Same sex pairs likely work best, but opposite sex pairs can work if you eliminate the romantic factor. Create three or four questions on the theme of the passage. If you're studying Galatians 6:1–5 you might choose: (a) Tell about a burden you bore (or would like to bear) for a friend; (b) Tell about a burden a friend bore for you (or that you would like that friend to bear); (c) Tell about a Christian action you can be proud of without comparing yourself to anyone else. Provide paper for each youth to write answers privately, guess the other's answers, and then reveal what they each wrote.

Talking in pairs helps each youth to find commonalities with another without the unnaturalness of being in front of the crowd. Follow up by inviting students to share one new way they've learned to live Galatians 6:1–5 (or whatever passage you're studying).

Old Temptation

In the childhood game, Old Maid, students take turns choosing a card from the other's hand, all the while trying to keep from ending up with the Old Maid card. Once they have two matching cards in their own hand, they lay those down. The Old Maid card has no match. Adapt this for youth Bible study by creating a single "old maid" that youth want to keep from, such as Tricky Temptation, Horrible Hypocrisy, or Lasting Loneliness. Then guide youth to create matches of actions that avoid that single card. Let youth make the cards, and then trade to play one another's games. Insist that they get both the "old maid" and the avoiding actions from the passage(s) you're studying—for temptation you might use Matthew 4 and include matches like *Quote Scripture* (Matt. 4:4); *Correct Misquotes* (Matt. 4:7); *Challenge Satan* (Matt. 4:10); *Accept God's Ministry* (Matt. 4:11). You could then follow up the game by discussing: With what masks do we pass temptation to others? How can we recognize temptation rather than step into its path? When do we want temptation, rather than avoid it? Why is temptation no game?

Pencil Charades

Popularized as Win/Lose/Draw and Pictionary, this method has broad appeal and focuses students on Scripture facts. It works well with any passage because students focus on finding the word-for-word phrases.

Process of Play

1. To prepare the **Pencil Charades** game, underline key phrases in the passage. Pay little attention to how easy the phrase is to draw. Youth have amazing drawing ideas and will watch the passage for clues.
2. Write each key phrase on a card. Bring a large pad and marker or a chalkboard and chalk.
3. Divide students into teams of about five. Shuffle the cards. Call for the student whose birthday is closest to begin.
4. Explain and play by the rules (below).

Rules

1. The person with the birthday closest to today goes first. This artist views a card with a Bible phrase written on it, and then draws the phrase for the team on a large pad with a marker (or on a chalkboard with chalk). Use drawings only, no numbers or words.
2. The phrase comes directly from Isaiah 53 (or whatever passage you're studying), so keep your Bibles open to Isaiah 53 while you guess.
3. Once a word is guessed, the artist can write that word above the drawing.
4. If the whole phrase is guessed within one minute, your team earns two hundred points. If guessed within two minutes, your team earns one hundred points.
5. There are no penalties for mistaken guesses.
6. Keep your Bibles open and encourage each other!

Follow-up

- This game works well as the "read the Bible passage" portion of the Bible study. Youth read the passage with intensity to draw and guess.
- After each correct guess, comment on the Bible phrase. This allows the game to become the vehicle for Bible examination.
- After the game, ask both fact and understanding questions about the passage to demonstrate how well students have learned it while playing the game.

Adaptations

- Rather than one team drawing at a time, guide teams to race by drawing simultaneously: Call an artist from each team. Show the artists the same phrase. On "Go!" artists return to their teams and draw on paper in the center of their circles. The first team to jump and shout the correct answer wins points. Again, stress open Bibles.
- Guide teams to create **Pencil Charade** cards (see "Process of Play") for other teams.
- Weekly ask your students to underline the three phrases in the Bible passage that they most want to remember. Then review the unit of study by drawing these phrases with **Pencil Charades**. Post the passage references so youth can leaf back and forth to them, but don't say which phrase came from which passage.
- Play acting charades instead of **Pencil Charades**.

Room-Size Bible Study Games

Room-size games are simply enlargements of board games or TV games. Keep the process of play, but take the questions from the Bible. A room-size game can be as quick as laying out several pieces of paper in a road and letting youth answer the question they land on. Or a room-size game can be as complex as creating an adaptation of a television game show complete with a huge spinner.

Adaptation: Use the actual game board, covering squares with your instructions and replacing game cards with Bible question cards.

Row

To guide a small group of students to digest blocks of content in your student book or Bible passage, play **Row**. This answering race is named for the rows in which youth sit. The object of this game is to reach and answer from the front row first.

Process of Play

1. Arrange the chairs in three rows of two chairs, facing the chalkboard or a sheet of paper or poster board on the wall.
2. This can be played with as few as three youth; two youth play against each other, and then the third youth enters to take the place of the winner of each round. If you have more than three youth, divide youth into two teams according to the date they were born; all born from the first through the fifteenth on one team, and all born from the sixteenth

through the thirty-first on another (or choose another team-forming method from chapter 16). Adjust by day until teams are even.

3. Call for one student from each team to sit in the back row, next to each other, with their student books open in their laps.
4. Explain the rules.
5. Remind youth the page in the student book from which you will ask the question. Ask a question that can be answered directly from the student book. You will have listed these questions ahead of time or underlined them. Ask questions in the order the answers appear in the content.
6. Say, "Move up one," to the youth who correctly completes the answer first. That youth will move to the chair directly in front of him. Repeat steps 5 through 6 until one youth answers correctly from the front chair. Ask questions in order of the way they appear in the content. Let students know when you move to a new page.
7. Let the first student to answer correctly from the front chair mark a point for his team on the poster hanging at the front of the rows.
8. If one student moves rapidly to the front, expect the other to move rapidly to the front during the next round. Encourage both students with comments like, "The answers are right there in the copy," or, "You can do it!" or, "Keep your finger on the former answer, and the next answer will be a line or two down."
9. Call for the next duo to race to the front row. You can choose a whole new pair or choose to let the runner-up try for first again. Just do the same thing every round (*Hint*: For students who answer more slowly, subtly encourage the Noisy Version explained in the Adaptations).

Rules

1. The object of this game is to read the passage in a fun way and find the answer to the question directly in the book. So keep your student book open to the assigned page. Don't try to do it from your head—look for the answers.
2. When it's your turn, sit next to your opponent in the back row.
3. As soon as you find the answer, speak it aloud and rapidly.
4. The first one to completely say the answer moves up one row. If your opponent starts before you, just talk faster.
5. You may choose to be coached by your team (this is the Noisy Version—see Adaptations), but the answer must come from your own mouth.

6. The first one to answer correctly from the front chair marks a point for his or her team.

Follow-up

- Highlight that the game helped your students read the passage to find facts. Transition to discussion by inviting each student to name one fact they learned during the game (this will likely be a question they answered). Urge them to read the Bible with similar goals: to find answers, to solve problems, to find out the specifics God shares.
- Explain that you will continue the study by finding out what the facts mean and how to apply them.

Adaptations

- Offer the Quiet Version or Noisy Version to each pair of competitors. In the Quiet Version, competitors find their own answers. In the Noisy Version, their teammates shout the answers and competitors repeat them. If one competitor wants Quiet and one wants Noisy, rearrange so two Noisys and two Quiets compete against each other.
- Play **Row** to digest a lengthy Bible passage, rather than a block of student-book commentary.
- The intent of this game is to find factual information that is printed in a block of copy. Follow it with opinion-sharing and discussion, but do not ask opinion and discussion questions during the course of the game.
- If your group is larger than six, set up three or four rows of three chairs to include more youth at once. Avoid playing with more than twelve students, so students have frequent turns.

Scripture Baseball

Similar to **Human Tic-Tac-Toe**, **Scripture Baseball** is played with people as markers; the baseball diamond is made of four chairs. Students choose whether to answer a single, double, or triple question. The advantage of **Scripture Baseball** is that youth can choose the difficulty of their question. Its disadvantage is that one youth must miss each inning for the game to work. Since we don't want to communicate that looking in the Bible is a way to miss answers, use a time limit to let youth race against the clock, and realize that with enough time they all would get the correct answer.

Process of Play

1. Arrange four chairs in the shape of a baseball diamond. Arrange remaining chairs in two groups, one group on each side of the diamond:

```
ᕼ ᕼ ᕼ            ᕼ            ᕑ ᕑ ᕑ
ᕼ ᕼ ᕼ          ᕼ   ᕼ          ᕑ ᕑ ᕑ
ᕼ ᕼ ᕼ            ᕼ            ᕑ ᕑ ᕑ
```

2. Get Bible questions on a single passage from your curriculum or write them yourself, writing the Bible verse reference and answer after each. Divide questions into singles, doubles, or triples depending on level of difficulty. (Sometimes singles have one answer, doubles have two, and triples have three answers.) Number the singles, number the doubles, and number the triples. [*Note:* Some groups choose more triples so they can say the question was too hard if they miss; other groups choose more singles, hoping to answer correctly. Write more of what your group likes.]

3. Form two teams with a neutral dividing method such as last digit of street address (see chapter 16 for more team-forming ideas). Seat teams on opposite sides of the baseball diamond.

4. Challenge each team to bat in as many runners as possible by answering Bible questions while racing against the clock. Explain they can do this with singles, doubles, or triples.

5. Explain that the game is open Bible—all answers come directly from the Bible passage. Post the Bible verses for easy reference.

6. Explain that there is a time limit and that without the time limit everyone would get the answers because they are in the Bible.

7. Explain and play by the rules below. Continue play until all questions are asked or time is up.

Rules

1. The batter with the birthday closest to today goes first. The batter chooses the level of difficulty (single, double, or triple) and sits in that chair with his Bible. To keep any from feeling favored by the questioner, the batter requests a Bible question by number. (*Option:* Omit this rule occasionally to gear questions to each student's ability.)

2. The team member must answer with no help from his team but with lots of help from his Bible. If he answers correctly, he stays in that chair. If not, he is out, and the other team is up. Repeat that the answers are in the Bible and that we find them by opening to the passage.

3. Allow only one out per inning to keep sides changing.

4. The other team must pay close attention while a batter is in the chair. If the batter misses, the opposing team may consult among themselves and send a batter to answer that same question (this helps both teams pay attention and look up all answers).

5. All batters ahead of a new batter advance as many chairs as the new batter; i.e., if one batter is on second and the new batter answers a double correctly, the second base batter moves to home.

6. No team member may play a second time before all play once.

7. The decision of the judge will be final.

8. Encouraging words to opposing teams may be rewarded with extra points.

Follow-up

• As questions are answered, highlight points about the Bible passage. Let discussion flow naturally from the game process.

• Challenge youth to reread the passage for a truth they are glad to know. Call for several to share the truth that they found and why they like it.

Adaptations

• The one disadvantage to **Scripture Baseball** is that someone has to miss for the other team to get a turn. Bolster the confidence of students who miss by talking about how hard the question was and reminding them that without the time limit they would get the answer. Also switch frequently so students can have at least two chances to be up at bat.

• If your room is too small for the chairs, make a baseball diamond with masking tape on the table, floor, or wall. Guide students to make paper images of themselves to run around the diamond.

Spoons

In **Spoons** youth sit in a circle with a set of spoons in the middle. The spoons are also in a circle. There should be one less spoon than students. Youth pass around cards one at a time, holding only four at a time, until they get four of a kind; the youth that gets four of a kind first can take a spoon. The others race to get the remaining spoons. For Bible Spoons the four matching cards might be a concept from the passage, a memory verse, a quality of love, and much more. As the cards pass through students' hands, they will memorize them.

Process of Play

1. Prepare a set of concepts or words that match your Bible passage. Then make four cards of each concept. A computer and printer can produce multiple copies on heavy stock. You might print the Beatitudes from Matthew 5, plagues from Exodus 7–11, or another set.
2. Shuffle the cards.
3. Seat youth in a circle with one less spoon than youth in the center.
4. Enlist the first youth to draw four cards from the stack, choose the three he wants to keep, discard one, pick up another, and continue discarding and picking another. The youth next to him follows the same process from his discards, being only four cards behind. And so on around the circle.
5. When any youth collects four of a kind, she furtively picks up a spoon.
6. When the rest of the players notice that the first player has picked up a spoon, all others pick up a spoon as fast as possible. The one without a spoon earns an *S*. If it happens again, a *P*, then an *O*, another *O*, and then an *N*.
7. Let a different youth start the card-passing each time.
8. When S.P.O.O.N. is spelled completely by one player, the game is over.

Rules

1. Open your Bible to the passage, and hold it open in your lap during the game.
2. Your goal is to collect four cards that match exactly.
3. When you get four, pick up a spoon.
4. If you haven't yet gotten four, and someone else picks up a spoon, pick up a remaining spoon as quickly as possible.
5. If you don't get a spoon, or if you pick up a spoon and you don't have a matching set, you gain a letter (*S,P,O,O,* or *N.*)
6. You must choose the top card.
7. You may not pick a card back up once it is discarded.

Follow-up

- Give each youth a set of four, and equip them to become the authority on that concept. For a plague, students might find it in Exodus 7–11, illustrate it, and give three facts about it. For a Beatitude, students could tell how God will bless us through that Beatitude. For any list, youth could read the Bible passage and related student-book commentary.

Adaptations

- Let youth make the Spoons cards.
- Spell something that matches your passage, such as P.L.A.G.U.E.

Squashed Together Letters

When you want students to remember a key phrase, a Bible verse, or a fact, squash all the letters together and challenge students to separate them. As they mark lines between each word, they remember each word.

These squashed together letters tell why Bible games work:

GAMESBUILDFAMILIARITYWITH-
SCRIPTUREYOUTHAREALREADYINTER-
ESTEDINGAMESCOMPETITION
MOTIVATESINVOLVEMENTGAMESWITH-
WELLTHOUGHTOUTRULESPROVIDEOP-
PORTUNITYTOBESMART
INTHEBIBLEMOVINGENCOURAGESAT-
TENTIONYOUTHDON'TREALIZETHEY'RELEARNING-
NEWBIBLE
KNOWLEDGESUCCESSBUILDSCONFI-
DENCEWITHSCRIPTURE

Stand When You Know

This expanded version of **Pop** (see chapter 6) guides students to find and answer Bible fact questions quickly. They also learn by writing questions for the game. The questions can be from the same passage, or each team can be the expert in a portion of a longer passage.

Process of Play

1. Divide your group into three or more teams using a team-forming method from chapter 16. Seat teams across from each other (in a triangle if three teams, square if four teams, pentagon if five, and so on).
2. Direct each team to write five questions based on the passage you assign. Emphasize that the answers must be in the Bible passage. Provide cards and pencils.
3. When the questions have been written, call for team *A* to read one of its questions. The first youth on an opposing team to stand and answer the question wins a point for his or her team.

4. Continue to team *B*, and so on. If any team presents a question that no other team can answer in sixty seconds, that team wins points for a stump.

Rules

1. To prevent one team from dominating the answering, no one team member can answer two questions in a row.
2. Let one neutral person watch to see who jumps first.
3. Insist that youth point in their Bibles to the answer. Otherwise they earn no points. This keeps their Bibles open, helps new Bible discovery happen, and keeps youth from guessing.

Follow-up

Affirm youth for writing biblically centered questions. Invite them to help you comment on the passage(s) using their student books.

Adaptation

Write the questions yourself prior to the session.

Trading Game

Popularized as Pit, the trading game guides youth to memorize lists of items in a Bible passage. Beginning with a set of cards that do not match, students trade to collect identical cards. While trading, students memorize the items that pass through their hands. Create a trading game with any list from the Bible. Examples include fruits of the Spirit (Gal. 5:22–23); characteristics of love (1 Cor. 13:4–7); Ten Commandments (Exod. 20:1–17).

Process of Play

1. List the actions, words, or characteristics you want to study.
2. Write each item on four cards. Four cards form a matching set.
3. Create a set of four cards for each youth with a photocopy machine or computer. Duplicate sets if you have more youth than words. Play twice if you have fewer youth than words.
4. When the youth have arrived, count out a set for each youth present. Shuffle the cards and distribute so each one has four nonmatching cards.
5. Explain the rules and play (below).
6. Call for youth to explain the item on their matching set, using the Bible passage and student-book commentary.

Rules
1. You have four nonmatching cards. Each is a fruit of the Spirit (or whatever list you have chosen). When I say "Go," obtain a set of four matching cards by trading one card at a time. Don't show the cards you trade.
2. You may find that someone else is trying to collect what you are trying to collect. Feel free to change to something else.
3. When you finish, find your characteristic in the Bible passage (or student book) and prepare to tell how to use it.
4. When you are prepared, help others trade until they all have matching sets.

Follow-up
- Call on the youth, one at a time, to name their fruit of the Spirit (or other list) and tell how living it would bring good to their school.
- Invite volunteers to recite all nine fruits of the Spirit (or other list).

Adaptations
- Give matching cards initially and instruct youth to trade until they have one each of different cards.
- The trading game also works well with theme studies. For example, four types of prayer are *praise*, *petition*, *confession*, and *intercession*.

Words Can't Say

Popularized as Taboo, youth prompt each other to guess certain words or phrases without saying the "can't-say" words. Because players can say all but the specified words, this game guides students to describe in detail biblical concepts such as salvation and sanctification. Here's a sample used in a Sunday school lesson on Ephesians 6:10–20:

Bible phrase to be guessed	Can't say these words
Belt of truth	waist, buckle, right
Breastplate of righteousness	shield, chest, protection
Feet fitted with readiness	shoe, sock, prepared
Shield of faith	metal, silver, barrier
Helmet of salvation	hat, head, believer
Sword of the Spirit	spear, sharp, Bible

Process of Play

1. Divide youth into partners according to last digit of phone number, or another team-forming method in chapter 16.
2. Prepare a set of three-by-five-inch cards with the Bible word to be guessed at the top and the can't-say words listed under it. Choose about three can't-say words for each. The goal is to get youth to describe rather than just give synonyms to the word.
3. Show one student the card so she or he can get the partner to say the Bible word without saying any of the can't-say words. Urge youth to look in the Bible passage for identifying words, explaining that this lets the Bible teach about the Bible.
4. Time each pair so they race against the clock.
5. Watch to make sure that no can't-say words are mentioned. Move on to the next pair if that happens.
6. After the word is guessed, prompt all youth to find it in their Bibles. Then give a sentence or two of explanation, or have the youth give it. In this way the game becomes the vehicle for Bible study.
7. Move on to a new pair after every word, rather than give the same pair another word. This gives all youth opportunity to shine frequently.

Rules

1. When it's your team's turn, look at the Bible word card and the can't-say words.
2. Use descriptions besides the can't-say words to get your partner to name the Bible word. You can use as many words as you want, but no gestures.
3. If you say a can't-say word, you forfeit your turn.
4. Work quickly, trying to get your partner to guess more quickly than any other team.
5. When your partner guesses the word, find it in today's Bible passage and hear its explanation from your teacher.
6. Move on to the next pair, encouraging them to guess quickly.
7. Always encourage your partner and the others playing.

Follow-up

Highlight that this game has helped us describe Bible words in detail. This helps us understand what the Bible means and how to apply it.

Adaptations

- Let the can't-say words be any churchese words, words Christians understand but nonbelievers might not understand.
- Let youth choose their own Bible words and can't-say words. Keep all students on a single Bible passage, the one you're studying that day.

Word That Definition

Mention a Bible dictionary, and most teenagers recoil. But this especially fun game makes teens want to seek and know definitions for Bible words. During the game students race to be the first to identify a Bible word that is being defined. This game starts slowly—it takes a few rounds for teens to catch on—but then it takes off like a rocket. And youth don't want to quit. "Just one more definition?" they'll beg.

Process of Play

1. As your students enter the room, direct them to one of at least three teams, according to a team-forming method in chapter 16. Three teams are needed so that two can compete against the third. If you have only three students, let each be a team.
2. Give each team one or more copies of a Bible dictionary that has been especially written for teenagers such as the *Holman Student Bible Dictionary*. Insure that each youth has a Bible.
3. Write on the chalkboard a single Bible passage and these instructions: "Underline or jot down at least ten words to define in this passage." For Romans 5 these words might include *justified, faith, peace, God, Lord, Jesus, Christ, grace, glory, ungodly, righteous, sinners, wrath, reconciled, rejoice, reconciliation,* and more.
4. Then direct students to complete these instructions: "Find each word in your Bible dictionary and mark it with slips of paper." Urge them to read each definition as they find it so they can identify it during the game.
5. When all groups have marked at least ten definitions, start the competitive part of the game. Say: "When I say 'Go,' stand to read one of the definitions you found. Don't say the word or any part of the word, just the definition. The first to stand and be called on reads a definition and wins a point. Then the first person from another team to stand and correctly identify the defined word from the Bible wins a point."

6. Say "Go!" Call on the first one standing to read the definition. Give that team a point.
7. Call on the first one standing from another team to identify the word. If correct, give that team a point. If not, call on the next one standing.
8. Repeat steps 6 and 7. After each word has been correctly named, comment briefly on its meaning in the passage. This makes the game a vehicle for Bible study.

Rules

1. Find at least ten words in your passage to define.
2. Use slips of paper to mark those definitions in your Bible dictionary.
3. Prepare to stand and read one of those definitions when the teacher says, "Go!" You'll earn a point for being the first one standing to read.
4. If you're not first to stand, your group can guess the word defined by another group. Be the first to stand and name the correct word for a point.
5. You cannot guess the word for a definition that is read by a member in your own group, even if you don't know ahead of time the word she or he defines.
6. Keep your Bible open to the passage to name the words. Don't guess.
7. Read all the definitions you find during the preparation steps 1 and 2 to make it easier to remember which definitions match which words.

Follow-up

- Let the Bible study take place during the game by highlighting a sentence or two of commentary about each named word. After the game, invite each youth to choose three words and put them in a single sentence to summarize the truth of the passage.
- Remember to stay in a single passage rather than try to define words from all over the Bible. The goal is to digest a single Bible passage.

Adaptations

- If no team can correctly identify a word after six tries, give the defining team an extra point for a stump. First, make certain the word is actually in the passage and that the definition can actually be found in the Bible dictionary.
- If you have only two youth, let them race against the clock to find the word after the other reads its definition. Follow the same process otherwise.

Plus . . .

Almost any game can be adapted for use in youth Bible study by substituting questions about the Bible passage for the questions in the game. These games have been successfully adapted for Bible study. How might you use these or something similar?

- Bible Bowl (like College Bowl quiz games with buzzers and teams)
- Slapjack (Slap cards that agree with the Bible passage)
- Tabletop Football (when you get a question right, you try for a touchdown)
- Bible Football (downs for correct answers)
- Catch Phrase (act out the phrase very rapidly)
- Guesstures (act out the phrase very rapidly)
- Simon Says (except change it to Jesus Says and quote from words of Jesus)
- Relay Race (run up, answer the question correctly, run back)
- Wheel of Fortune (a fancy version of **Hangman** in which you buy the vowels)
- Family Feud (family groups compete to answer Bible questions)
- Mad Libs (substitute random words for parts of speech in the story)
- Ungame, Sorry, Monopoly, and other board games
- What's My Line? (good for studying Bible characters)
- Fruit Basket Turnover (key Bible phrases get everyone moving)
- Twenty Questions (ask up to 20 yes-or-no questions to get everyone moving)
- H.O.R.S.E. (basketball one-on-one game; correct answers give a chance to shoot)
- Jigsaw Puzzles (good for studying the body of Christ or for assembling a portion of Scripture)
- Pin the Tail on the Donkey (closest one to the tail gets to answer the question)
- Three-Legged Race (tie partners together by the arm or leg so they can work as a team to pool their resources in answering Bible questions)

Chapter 6

❧❧

Creative Questioning

Good questions motivate youth to search the Bible, not guess what's in your head.

Rationale: Most teachers include questions and answers in every session. It's a wonderful and brilliant process that guides students from fact learning to fact understanding. Question-and-answer has so many variations that it never has to grow old.

How can you maintain the good in this tried-and-true method? Simply vary the way you ask questions—there are more than two dozen variations in this chapter. Then wait for your students to answer, rather than fill in your own blanks.

What if you ask a question and everyone just sits there or one student answers all the questions? Use question formats that require all youth to answer or that make all youth feel comfortable talking. **Under Chair Questions**, **Alphabetical Answers**, and similar processes get all youth involved in the learning. Each is described in this chapter.

How can we help our students want to answer? Treasure what each teenager says so they'll want to talk more. Even the most off-the-wall response can be greeted with a genuine, "I'm glad you spoke up. Which verse led you to that conclusion?"

Teaching Tip: Make it probable that youth will succeed at answering questions. Do this by starting with questions that can be answered directly from the Bible passage. Then gently move youth forward to application questions, still drawing on Bible verses for ideas. Success with God's Word, not ranking kids in answering ability, is our goal. As youth have success with Bible questions, they trust the Bible and their ability to obey it.

Teaching Tip: When youth ask questions you don't know how to answer, refuse to panic. Calmly explain that you don't know the answer, but you will find out. This communicates three important truths: (1) teachers are still learning; (2) Christians don't have to have all the answers because God has the answers; (3) some answers take time to find, and as we persist we can find those answers.

Teaching Tip: Let your students know when an assignment is hard so they won't feel stupid for struggling with it.

Teaching Tip: Keep the answer source apparent. When youth have an answer source, they can find the answers. Usually this source will be the Bible; other times it will be commentary about the Bible; occasionally it will be the youth's own experience. Post the reference to keep students on track.

Alphabetical Answers

Give each pair of students a copy of the alphabet printed down the left side of the paper. Students then are to give you twenty-six answers to your question, each beginning with a different letter of the alphabet. If you've been studying John and your assignment is characteristics of Jesus, answers might include: **A**ll the world was made through Jesus; **B**efore Jesus came, John prepared the way; **C**an bring light into darkness; **D**arkness can't understand him; **E**ven though he was the light, the world did not recognize him; **I**n him is life; etc.

Another Choice

Youth too frequently think they have no choice in what happens to them. To show that they always have more than one choice, guide youth to suggest two choices they have related to the passage. Make this more intriguing by insisting they use the same letter to begin each choice: "I can _____ instead of _____." For example, to obey Ephesians 4:29 they can <u>a</u>ct instead of <u>a</u>rgue; <u>g</u>reet nicely instead of show <u>g</u>rouchiness; <u>w</u>ind up telling the problem instead of <u>w</u>hine.

Ask: "Why do you always have more than one choice? How does thinking through your options ahead of time guide you to please God in every choice, to do good on purpose so bad won't happen by accident?"

Adaptation: Expand to more than two choices.

Answer Options

Some youth are comfortable with words. Others, equally smart, would rather doodle or demonstrate their answer. Still others want to tell a story that shows an example. Offer at least two ways to respond to any question you ask: draw or say, doodle or write, give an example or illustrate, choose a word or symbol, speak or sketch, write a song or quote a song.

Between a Rock and a Hard Place

Invite youth to talk about their dilemmas before they get into them (or before they get into them again) so they'll be ready to face them. Invite the students to tell about a time they were (or will be) between a rock and a hard place and which way God wants them to move. The format is "I was caught between _____ and _____ and God guided me to _____ to get out of it." For example:

- Tell about a time you were caught between a friend and a parent.
- Tell about a time you knew what to do but didn't have the courage.
- Tell about a time you wanted to submit but felt too proud.
- Tell about a time you felt pulled by your hormones and your brain.
- Tell about a time you wanted to know someone but feared taking the risk.
- Tell about a time you wanted to encourage someone but didn't.

Churchy to Concrete

Teenagers know the church routine—that churchy answers will satisfy many teachers. The standard five are: "go to church," "read your Bible," "pray," "love one another," and "witness." Those five will accurately answer many questions, but they don't show youth how or why to do these things. So guide youth beyond general answers to specific ones. A question that works in most cases is: "Give me an action, attitude, or sentence that would show that in your life." Here are some other samples:

- "With what action would you show you love someone?"
- "What is the first sentence you'd pray?"
- "What facial expression shows patience?"
- "What words deny compassion? What words show it?"
- "What attitude would show you have forgiven someone?"

Caution: A student once came to me upset because I had rejected her churchy answer. She rightly concluded that prayer was the right answer, and I had asked for something else. She taught me to say, "Yes, that's right. But give me more detail. What sentence would you say, in a prayer about this?" We must not communicate that the one-word answers are wrong but that we need to add the detail that shows us how to live that answer (see **Commandment V** in chapter 3).

Adaptation: Alert youth to supportively call out "churchy answer" when someone gives an answer that is true but shows more talk than walk.

Compare

Comparison helps students notice how and why Bible truth works. Here are three of the many ways to compare:

1. Guide students to compare the Bible passage to something that happens today: "If Jesus gave a Sermon on the Mount (Matt. 5–7) at your school today, what would he emphasize?"
2. Guide students to compare a Bible character to themselves or a presently famous person: "I avoid King David's mistake by . . ."
3. Guide students to compare how life is easier when persons let God give them courage to obey his commands: "Compare how Peter was before Jesus was crucified and how he was after Jesus was crucified."

Create Quizzes

Challenge pairs of students to create quizzes with five questions based on the passage you are studying. For long passages, assign each pair to a different section of the Bible commentary. Agree on a format for quizzes such as true/false, multiple choice, fill-in-the-blank, one-word answer, multiword answer, matching, or mazes. Then exchange and solve, perhaps using one of the learning game formats in chapter 5.

Five Solutions

While discussing what to do about a dilemma, guide students to list three to five possible solutions, and then take turns telling an advantage and a disadvantage of each solution. Finally, encourage them to make a decision. This guides students to look at decisions more completely. It also helps students see that all solutions cost but that God's solutions pay benefits far greater than any cost. Example:

Dilemma: *Should I have sex before marriage?*

- Possibility 1: Yes, because I am in love.
  Advantage: Can express my love physically; feels good.
  Disadvantage: Destroys even a good relationship.
- Possibility 2: No, because God said so.
  Advantage: Feel good about decision and relationship with God; builds stronger relationship with my date.
  Disadvantage: Get labeled a prude or a cold fish.

- Possibility 3: Yes, because most other people do.
  Advantage: Get lots of dates.
  Disadvantage: Get a bad reputation.
- Possibility 4: Yes, because I don't want to spoil the romance.
  Advantage: My date wants to also.
  Disadvantage: Could get AIDS, get pregnant, or get dumped.
- Possibility 5: No, for the sake of my happiness in marriage.
  Advantage: I'll know my spouse and I share something we never shared with anyone else.
  Disadvantage: Hard to wait until marriage.

Decision: I will wait because true love waits. The advantage is that even if I marry the one I'm dating now, I give a gift by waiting.

Variation: Use this with television shows. Rather than ask, "Is this a good show?" invite students to name three advantages and three disadvantages.

Guys, Then Girls

Let the guys answer one question as a group, then the girls; the next time start with the girls. The need to defend honor before the opposite sex prompts students to do their best. Also the teamwork pools wisdom and keeps one student from doing all the answering.

Hot Bag

Any time your curriculum or plan includes a series of questions, cut them apart and place them in a brown paper lunch sack to play Hot Bag. Twist the top of the sack and pass it around your circle like a hot potato. Direct youth to pass the bag until the music stops, skipping no one and holding the bag for no one. With your back turned, play music or hum "Jesus Loves Me." Stop at an unexpected place. When the music stops, the student holding the bag must draw out a question and answer it. Encourage youth to keep their Bibles open in their laps to find the answer quickly. Repeat.

This simple bag method adds great motivation for finding Bible answers. The process is also valuable for sharing solutions to problems in the bag. Avoid pandemonium with rules like "Pass the bag at a steady pace" and "Pass to the person next to you rather than across the circle."

I Was There

Direct youth to answer questions from the point of view of one character in the passage you are studying. Perhaps during the fiery furnace incident they might be Shadrach, Meshach, Abednego, the angel, a soldier, an onlooker, or King Nebuchadnezzar (Dan. 3). Call on youth to say what they see, feel, hear, think, and, in some instances, smell and taste.

Variation: Provide name tags to help youth recall who is who.

Variation: Use this with theme studies to represent various points of view. During a study on witnessing, one youth can be skeptical, one rebellious, one open, and so on.

Life Questions

Relate your questions to life as much as possible. Listen to what your students talk about before and after class, and gear your questions to these issues. Some classics:

- How does this verse impact how we relate to our parents? How we'd like them to relate to us?
- Tell about a mistake you made. How can this verse help you fix it? Avoid it?
- What was the hardest decision you ever made? What light does this verse shed?
- How do you know God is real?
- What worries you?
- Name a best friend. How could obeying this verse help you stay close?
- How does this verse help you choose your friends?
- What help would this verse give when a friend lets you down?
- How will that choice affect you? The other people involved?
- What will happen if you do this verse? If you don't?
- How would the world be affected if everyone did this verse?
- Why does God ask us to do this/not do this?
- What will be gained/lost by doing this? By doing something else?

List a Lot

List a Lot generates spur-of-the-moment answers and then rejects those answers that don't match God's solutions. Guide youth to list rapidly, and out loud, every possible solution to a problem or question and to refrain from evaluating them until all ideas are down. Then, as a group, evaluate each answer and choose one. Listing first reminds youth not to cross off any idea initially. Evaluating at the end reminds youth to think through every possibility before trying a specific one. Because all participants shout answers at the same time, youth feel more comfortable joining in the listing. Because tons of ideas are listed, the best solution becomes easier to find.

Accept and write on large paper all answers, even those you know to be off the wall. This helps students know you are listening and gives them courage to say more honest answers. Then evaluate the final list with questions like "Which of these are most likely to work according to the Bible and why? Which are least likely to work according to the Bible and why? Does God want you to do this one? Why or why not? How are God's ways the most practical of all?"

New Example

To encourage a plethora of applications, insist that each youth give a different example of how to apply the passage you are studying. Make it taboo to say "I agree with what she said." Of course youth want to affirm each other's ideas but not use them as excuses to omit their own Bible insights.

Point to the Answer

As you ask fact questions about the Bible, instruct students to keep their Bibles open. Explain that to be correct, they must put their finger on the word or phrase that confirms their answer. This motivates them to search their Bibles rather than just guess.

Pop

Especially good for small groups, **Pop** challenges youth to be the first one standing when you ask a question. Once you've asked your Bible question, wait a few seconds to give everyone a chance to find it and then say "Pop." The first youth standing gets to answer the question.

Adaptation: If you have a student who can't stand quickly, let the pop action be something every one can do such as hold up a card, flop a head down, or sneeze.

Adaptation: Let the first student standing ask the next Bible question. This guides them to stay even more involved with the Bible passage because they put it into question form.

Questions in New Places

Vary the places you put questions to invite every student to talk. Consider these possibilities:

- A question on the back of each student. Students mingle, answering the question for each other without telling what the question is. The wearer of the question tries to figure out the question on his back as well as answer other students' questions.
- A question composed by each student, handed to the left, answered on paper and then passed again. Instead of numbering these one through ten, number them Amber to Zach, depending on the names of your students.
- A series of questions in a box to draw like a prize.
- A different question on each candy wrapper; a student must answer before eating the candy.
- A different question inside each balloon to pop and find.
- A series of questions on a cough drop box when studying care during illness.
- A series of questions on tissues when discussing crying along with fellow Christians during sad times (Rom. 12:15).
- A question under each chair (see **Under Chair Questions** below).
- A series of questions to be played back one at a time (see **Tape-Recorded Questions** below).

Riddles

Create, or guide youth to create and exchange, riddles that have their answers in the Bible passage you are studying. The riddles may rhyme, but they don't have to. Examples for the tower of Babel (Gen. 11:1–9):

1. Thought it would make a name

   Seemed obsessed with fame

   God saw the danger in this power

   And he took away this tower.
2. What planned to reach the heavens but heaven reached down to it?

Scavenger Hunt

Give each team a list of things to find in a Bible passage. This is especially helpful for long passages such as the story of Joseph or when studying an entire book of the Bible. Youth won't want to read it straight, but searching for scavenger hunt items results in their digesting the passage. Pairs work especially well with this type of assignment; larger groups tend to let one or two do all the work.

To make the hunt more challenging, do not give verse numbers. If you want the activity to go quickly, keep the items in the order they appear in the text or give the verse ranges. A sample of items to find from the Book of Galatians *(sources in italics; do not give to students):*

1. The author of Galatians *(1:1)*
2. Reason Galatians was written *(1:6–7)*
3. Number of years Paul stayed in Damascus *(1:17–18)*
4. Man called an apostle to the Jews *(2:8)*
5. Why the law was put in charge *(3:23–24)*
6. Three divisions that no longer exist in Christ Jesus *(3:28)*
7. Name for God that means "daddy" *(4:6)*
8. The time it is fine to be zealous *(4:17–18)*
9. Nine fruits of the Spirit *(5:22–23)*
10. Two things to do when a burden exists *(6:2, 5)*

Students Ask the Questions

A successful way to involve youth is to let them be the authority. Give one student your questions (with the answer key), and invite him or her to ask the class the questions. Alternate "teachers" every few questions.

Talk Around the Circle

Invite participation with a rule that everyone in the circle must add something new to the discussion. Whoever can't think of a new contribution in fifteen seconds has to stand until the next round. Let the assignment match your passage. This method is effective with both fact-finding and Bible application. It helps youth pay attention to what the other has said. And it has several inviting variations:

- *Group Story.* Each student adds another detail to a story. Example: "Chris Christian went to school planning to fight temptation. . . ." The details can be solutions, new wrinkles, and more.
- *Answer by Name.* Each student gives an answer beginning with the first letter of his name. Example: "I'm Susan, and I resist temptation by Staying away."
- *Answer by Verse.* Each student adds another detail from the passage. If you are listing characteristics of love from 1 Corinthians 13, each youth adds another characteristic and tells how to live it.
- *Answer Repeat.* Students remember one another's suggestions by repeating all those that came before and then saying their own answers.

The second youth repeats what the first said before saying hers. The third repeats what the first and second said, and so on.

Tape-Recorded Questions

Enlist a person besides yourself to tape-record the questions for that day's passage. Ask that the questioner leave a few seconds of silence between questions. During the Bible study, direct students to pass the recorder, play one question, answer it from the Bible, and pass it to the next student. The novelty of the tape recorder invites youth's attention and interest. Other times they get carried away trying to discover who is speaking. If this happens, spend a few moments guessing until the identity is confirmed.

Under Chair Questions

Any time you have a series of questions to answer, tape one under each chair before students arrive. Then when the time comes for question-and-answer, challenge kids to remove the question from under their chair and find the answer in the Bible passage. This method encourages every youth to talk and prevents one from dominating the question/answer time.

Adaptation: Save writing time by cutting the questions out of your teacher's book. If you prefer keeping your book intact, duplicate the page and cut apart the duplication.

Walk and Find

Create a hunt in which youth must search the room to find the questions and then search the Bible to find the answers. This is different from a **Scavenger Hunt** (see above) because youth sit still in the **Scavenger Hunt.** Students walk around the room in **Walk and Find**. Both methods have students seek answers in the Bible, but for **Walk and Find** students must also find the question. Show the location of the first question, and explain that it gives a clue for the location of the next question, which gives a clue for the next question, and so on. Give your students paper, and challenge them to find the questions and then write the answer to each question from the Bible onto their paper. Find your questions in your curriculum, or write them from the Bible passage, including references. Post your questions separately in places like the following (this sample studies 1 John 1:1–10):

- *Question #1:* Write four characteristics of the Word (1 John 1:1).
  Look for your next question under the window.

- *Question #2:* Why did John proclaim what he had seen and heard? (1 John 1:3)

  Look for your next clue on the ceiling.
- *Question #3:* What is the message John proclaimed? (1 John 1:5)

  Look for your next clue under a table.
- *Question #4:* How can you tell if you have fellowship with God? (1 John 1:6–7)

  Look for your next clue by the chalkboard.
- *Question #5:* Can a Christian claim to be without sin? (1 John 1:8)

  Look for your next clue on your teacher's back.
- *Question #6:* What two things does God do when you confess your sin to him? (1 John 1:9)

  Look for your next clue on the floor.
- *Question #7:* Write about a sin you confessed and the change God brought in your life as a result (or write about a sin you need to confess). You may share your answer or keep it private.

  Congratulations! Take a seat in the circle of chairs.

Youth Say

To begin a Bible discussion, to share on controversial topics, or to name ways to apply a Bible passage, encourage youth to share their opinions with the question starter, "What do youth think about . . .?" Jesus used this technique in Matthew 16:13–20: He began by asking his disciples what other people said about him and then asked their own viewpoint. Frequently when you ask, "What do youth say/think/feel about . . ." youth give their own opinion.

Once students share their opinions, help them evaluate and refine them according to the Bible. Do this not by rejecting opinion, but by asking questions like, "How do our opinions match this Bible passage? How would Jesus shape our opinions to become more true to life? True to real love? True to truth?"

Plus . . .

Consider these other options for question-and-answer:
- Sealed orders consisting of Bible questions that youth complete privately and independently. These are frequently used for personal devotions at retreats.
- Give a headline or title to the Bible passage.
- Provide a question box for anonymous questions or for suggestions.

- Pretend to be a counselor, and give advice to the Bible character.
- Write questions on footprints that lead into your Bible study room to encourage youth to begin thinking about the topic you're studying.
- Play **Bible Jeopardy** (see chapter 5) or simply use the format of giving answers to elicit questions.
- Ask questions in any other game format (see chapter 5 for ideas).

Chapter 7

❦

Writing, Drawing, Word Puzzles, and More

*Use both words and drawings to
express Bible understanding.*

Rationale: When students put Bible insights onto paper they solidify vague ideas and express thoughts they hesitate to say out loud. Paper is private enough to encourage honesty and familiar enough that most youth feel safe venturing it. Youth who feel more comfortable writing thoughts than saying them may feel freer to share once they have written their ideas.

Make this Bible learning method even more appealing by adding drawing as an option. Drawings can communicate Bible truth even better than words. Both words and pictures demonstrate youth's understanding of the Bible passage. Cultivate the habit of offering two choices with every assignment: "draw or write," "jot down or doodle," "put into words or illustrate."

Teaching Tip: Let youth know, before they write or draw, how much they will be asked to share of what they put down. This lets them decide what to put. Private response encourages honest sharing between the student and God but can keep some students from working as hard. Shared response helps all grow from the others' insights but may keep some from writing honestly. Consider the happy medium of anonymous response or sharing some, but not all, of what is written.

Teaching Tip: Vary the shape, texture, or size of your paper to take away school transfer and add interest. Youth get so tired of worksheets and written homework that they resist it anywhere but school (and sometimes at school!) The more unusual your paper and the more interesting your assignment, the more youth will pay attention to and learn from it. Your local printer may give you scraps in a wide variety of colors and sizes. Avoid white 8-1/2-by-11-inch paper. Consider using papers that have interesting qualities:

- Colored
- Recycled
- Bumper stickers
- Long and thin
- Fragile
- Mirror paper (Mylar)
- Bookmarks

- Bumpy
- Round
- Stick-on notes
- Short and fat
- Heavy
- Business cards
- Tiny

- Sticky
- Square
- Stapled like books
- Oversized
- Bandages
- Cut in strips
- Cut in the shape of your theme

At times use no paper at all: Write on clay to simulate clay tablets. Find huge leaves to approximate papyrus. Write on light bulbs with glass markers when studying Jesus as the light of the world. Write Bible principles on hands as though preparing notes for the tests of life.

Teaching Tip: Take advantage of ways youth already write: phone numbers, notes to pass, diary entries, doodles, T-shirts, and more. To make the writing meaningful, always relate it both to the Bible passage and to real life. Use questions like "How has this writing/drawing made the Bible's truth more clear? How has it shown how you can live the Bible at school? How does it invite friends to become interested in living Christ's way?"

Acrostic

An acrostic uses the letters of the alphabet or a word to recall characteristics of that word or theme. Psalm 119 is an acrostic of the Hebrew alphabet, each section beginning with the next letter of the Hebrew alphabet. Readers of Hebrew remember the points by going through the alphabet or the acrostic word.

To do an acrostic, give youth the word and direct them to find in the Bible passage elements that begin with each letter. Examples: Beginning with each letter of H.U.M.I.L.I.T.Y. define *humility* with a phrase from Philippians 2. Beginning with each letter of your name, state a way you can show you are a Christian. Refer to James 1:19–27 for ideas.

Adaptation: Rather than write the acrostic on a single paper, cut the acrostic's letters from half sheets of paper and give each youth one. They write on the letter and then assemble the letters into words.

Adaptation: See **Alphabetical Answers** in chapter 6 for an alphabet acrostic.

Advice Letters

Guide students to write "Dear _____" letters asking advice for problems related to the passage you're studying. Then shuffle the letters, redistribute, and guide students to write advice, quoting at least once from the Bible passage. The advice-giver reads the problem and advice, to the group, and then invites other ideas. Youth love to get one another's advice, so this process tends to be instantly successful. Use it in the application portion of your study.

Variation: Challenge students to pretend they are Satan and write a letter tempting youth to do a specific wrong or avoid a specific right. Exchange and resist the temptation with specific strategies, quoting from Scripture at least once.

Awards

Guide youth to make certificates, buttons, bookmarks, or other award papers that show appreciation for a spiritual action. For example, while studying the fruits of the Spirit, classmates give each of the others an award for the fruit they see most often exhibited in that classmate's life. While studying temptation, classmates give each of the others an award for a specific way they watched that classmate resist temptation.

Option: Provide ribbons and seals to make the awards official looking. These are available in office supply stores.

Bracelet Commitment

"Fix these words of mine in your hearts and minds; tie them as symbols on your hands and bind them on your foreheads," says Deuteronomy 11:18. A physical reminder of a spiritual truth can help youth remember to do the good they want to do. For a time youth wore "What Would Jesus Do?" bracelets for this purpose. Guide your students to make a similar commitment band on the passage you're studying. Include the Scripture reference. Use heavy paper or cloth, writing with markers or fabric paints. Students can use short phrases such as "Ask Each Hour—Prov. 3:5–6" to remind themselves to acknowledge God so he can direct them. They could also use initials such as BQBPC-M6:1 for **Be Q**uietly **B**ut **P**ersistently **C**hristian based on Matthew 6:1.

Variation: Rings or armbands serve a similar purpose.

Break Replacement

To guide youth to focus on the words of a Bible passage, break the words incorrectly. Then guide students to put the breaks back where they go. This is supereasy to prepare on your computer; in fact your students will enjoy making them for the rest of the class.

1. First type the verse(s) correctly with the Bible reference.
2. Change the case to all capitals.
3. Close up all the words by deleting the spaces.
4. Put new spaces in.
5. Print.

A sample:

F ORG ODS OL OVE DT HEW OR LDJ OHN 3:16

Insist that students check the accuracy of their break replacements with their own Bibles. As they do, they will learn the verse word for word and grow ready to understand what each word means.

Buttons

Make button forms from circles of poster board or sticky paper. Give each student one on which to summarize the truths of the passage they have studied. Sample assignments:

- If Jesus (or other Bible person) wore a button, what would it say?
- What does this passage make you want to do?
- What does this passage make you want to be like?
- What attitude does this passage promote?

Guide students to wear the buttons to church, attach them to their Bibles, put them on their coats, or post them at home.

Charts

Charts can make complex truths clear by showing differences and similarities. A chart could show divisions between right and wrong, helpful and destructive, Christian and non-Christian. Possibilities for group charts:

- Qualities of the old life vs. qualities of the new life
- Reactions of the thieves on either side of the cross of Jesus
- Events that happened during each period in Bible history

Possibilities for individual charts:

- Chart your spiritual growth, labeling ups and downs.

- Chart your week, labeling times you lived for Christ and times you ignored him.
- Write what you want to be doing in ten years on the right side of your paper. Then illustrate, in order, the steps to get there.

Interesting formats for charts:

- Flip charts (open them up to find question/truth inside)
- Strip charts (open them to the side to find the question/truth inside)
- Banners (long, with large letters to focus on the theme)
- Cling charts (like flannel boards—add and remove items)
- Column charts (each column adds to/expounds on the previous one)
- Put together posters (involves students as they assemble)
- Words that wind, go upside down, or otherwise invite youth to follow

Adaptation: Youth may get bored with charts if only one or two write on it at a time. Solve this by laying the chart across the table or floor and giving everyone a marker or by cutting the chart apart and guiding teams to work in categories.

Circled Letters

This word game appears in some newspapers. It begins with four or five fill-in-the-blank questions. Each word blank consists of letter-length blanks with some letter blanks circled. After you fill in the correct word, its circled letters then unscramble to produce a key Bible truth or quote. The circled letters in these five answers unscramble to make the phrase: "God created fun."

1. What we eat three meals a day: Ⓞ Ⓞ O D
2. The talking device that connects us to other houses: P H O Ⓝ Ⓔ
3. What I do to learn what the Bible says: R Ⓔ A Ⓓ
4. How I can show you what I learned in the Bible: Ⓡ E P O R Ⓣ
5. What I send when you are sick or having a birthday: Ⓒ Ⓐ R Ⓓ s
6. The opposite of beautiful: Ⓤ Ⓖ L Y

To make a **Circled Letter** puzzle, write your Bible truth first and then use those letters in words that become the answers to four or five questions. If you can, let those questions be directly from the Bible passage. Write a space for each letter of each answer. Circle spaces for letters that will be used for unscrambling to become the Bible truth. Challenge students to fill in the blanks and unscramble the circled letters to discover the key Bible truth.

Crossword Grid

A crossword grid is a crossword puzzle without definition clues. Like a crossword puzzle, the words must correctly share letters, and crossword grids work best when all students have access to the same Bible translation (a good time to use printed Scripture in your student book). Unlike the crossword puzzle, the clues are Bible verse words themselves. Youth place every word of the verse or verses into the grid. Fitting the words to the grid encourages youth to read the verse repeatedly and to memorize it.

To prepare a crossword grid:

1. Write the words of the verse in order from longest to shortest.
2. Arrange the words on graph paper so each crosses with another, beginning with the longest word and moving toward the shortest. If words don't fit, skip them and come back when you see opportunity.
3. Rewrite the grid with no letters filled in. Duplicate.

This sample guides memory of Matthew 22:39:

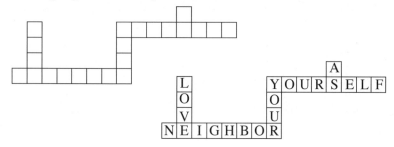

Crossword Puzzle

This familiar procedure appeals to youth because they know how to do it and because of its mystery element. A crossword puzzle is just as it sounds: words cross each other and share letters. Shared letters give clues to the other word(s). Definition clues also help discover the words. The best Bible crossword puzzles draw words and clues directly from the Bible passage or explanatory material students are studying. Crossword puzzles work best when all students have access to the same Bible translation. This is a good time to use printed Scripture in your student book. To enhance crossword puzzles:

• Race in pairs to see who can finish first.
• Let each student give one answer and tell why that fact matters.
• Enlarge the puzzle so it covers the floor or table.

- Guide youth to create their own crossword puzzles and exchange with each other. Youth will learn first by searching for clues to write and second by answering each other's crossword puzzles.

To create a crossword puzzle:

1. Circle key words in the passage (or commentary) youth will study.
2. Write a brief definition for each word.
3. Arrange the words on graph paper so that they cross, beginning with the longest word and moving toward the shortest word (if at first you don't succeed, keep rearranging). Put one letter in each square.
4. Label the definitions in order, arranged ACROSS and DOWN.
5. Recopy the crossword puzzle with no words filled in. Duplicate.

Hint: Many computer programs make crossword puzzles and then allow you to print as many copies as you need.

Crossword Reverse

Rather than find the crossword answers, guide youth to write the crossword clues. Give youth the crossword puzzle filled in, but the clue lines blank. Explain that their task is to write clues for each word. Then guide them to the Bible passage, student-book commentary, and Bible dictionary for information with which to write the clues for ACROSS and DOWN.

Decode by Telephone Pad

Guide youth to put a Bible truth into code according to the touchpad or rotary dial of a telephone. Then trade and solve each other's codes. The first number tells the key and the second tells which of the trio of letters to pick. Jesus is coded: 5-1 3-2 7-3 8-2 7-3. Pre-insert Q and Z for any words that use those letters. Have telephones handy for youth to reference as they decode. Or draw out an illustration of a telephone touchpad or a rotary dial.

Adaptation: You make the code, and let students solve it as they arrive, for a motivation to enjoy the Bible study. The advantage of students making the coded messages is that they will remember them as they write them; the advantage of your making the coded messages is that students will be drawn immediately into finding the answer.

Decode the Truth

Middle schoolers are particularly fond of decoding and mystery solving. Watch for decoding ideas in newspapers, on cereal boxes, and in contests. Then write or draw the Bible truths in those formulas. Even better, guide students to create coded messages for each other based on the Bible passage. Try these possibilities:

- *A=Z:* Youth write A through Z in one column and then Z through A in the other column. The matching letters give the code. Any shifting of letters provides a similar code.
- *Backwards Words:* Youth must translate words written backwards into forward-written words or hold them to a mirror to read them. This gives quick results.
- *Circled Code:* Draw several intersecting circles; and write a number in each circle. Then write an alphabet letter in each section, including the intersecting sections. Your code becomes the numbers that correspond to the letters you want. Numbers in intersecting parts are the two circle numbers added together.
- *Picture Code:* Put tiny pictures under each letter. Your code becomes the pictures that students translate back into the letter.
- *Tic-Tac-Toe Code:* Make three tic-tac-toe boards with nine letters of the alphabet in each. The first tic-tac-toe set contains just the letters, the second adds a dot in each box, and the third adds a line in each box. Then spell words with portions of those tic-tac-toe boards. Jesus would be spelled like this:

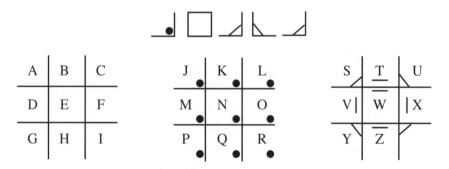

Decoder Wheel

In a circle of letters, youth write the arrowed letter and then every second letter to find a secret message. This sample gives a secret to getting along with parents. Students use the lines in the center of the wheel, writing one letter on each line.

Define by Sorting

To guide students to define tough concepts, give a list of actions, and direct students to sort them according to the concept you want them to learn. They can sort sin from not sin, Christlikeness from not Christlikeness, earthly from heavenly, loving from hateful, mercy from selfishness, and more.

Diary Entries

Youth put their most private thoughts into diaries or journals. Invite them to do the same during Bible study. Direct them to choose a character in the story and write a diary entry, telling the events from that person's point of view. Or direct them to be themselves and journal how the passage impacts them today or in the future. This choose-a-character-in-the-story sample was written by a tenth-grade boy during a study of Daniel:

> Dear Diary,
>
> I am a friend of someone who broke the law, but since I signed that paper that those "yes-men" gave me, my friend has to spend the night in the pit with the lions. I can't believe I signed knowing of my friend's religious ties. It looks like I'm going to have to break my own law and pray for my friend's safety. I'm going to check on him now diary, so wish me luck. — The King

Doorknob Message

To enable your students to see a Bible message daily, direct them to write it on a doorknob hanger. Cut these from heavy paper such as poster board, each about 8 1/2 inches by 3 1/2 inches, the size of one-third of a page. Cut a circle for the doorknob stem, with a sideways slit to attach it. A sample doorknob message would be "God saw all that he had made, and it was very good" (Gen. 1:31). This reminds students to live their value in God. Give students the paper and say: "Write on this paper a quotation from the passage, then a sentence or picture that reminds you how to live this Bible passage." Urge youth to hang these on their bedroom doors to prompt them to put God's Word into practice.

E-mail Address

Challenge students to compose an E-mail address that expresses their commitment to live a specific Bible truth that you have studied that day. Limit each students to ten characters (or the current E-mail maximum length).

E-mail Message

Draw, print, or ask students to compose an E-mail form on paper. Direct students to write on that form an E-mail message to a friend explaining what they discovered about the day's Bible passage. Ban them from using any "churchy" words (words only someone in church would understand). Encourage them to use E-mail symbols such as **:-**) for a smile.

Adaptation: Use actual computers and send the E-mails to each other to reinforce the lesson.

Adaptation: Use E-mail to send each of your students a question about the Bible study to prompt them to begin thinking about the Bible theme. Send this a day or two ahead of the Bible study *or* send a follow-up question to encourage application. Mail the message to any without on-line access.

Epic Poem

Youth who take classics at school will recognize epic poems as long stories told in poetry form. Those who read storybooks as children will recognize "Casey at the Bat" as a modern-day epic poem. Guide students to tell the Bible events in epic poem format, quoting part of the day's passage in many of the lines. Remember to stay with a single passage or a series of related passages.

Fake Money

Use play money or invite an artistic youth to draw obviously fake $1, $10, $100, and $1,000 bills for Bible study. Duplicate them on green paper, and use them to study 1 Timothy 6:6–10 ("the love of money is a root of all kinds of evil"), for a study on stewardship, or for a study on use of physical resources. Handling and "spending" the money will add more focus on the study.

Find the Impostor

Give youth a list of commonly quoted verses related to your theme, only some of which come from the Bible. Challenge youth to find the impostors by looking up the verse references you supply. There will be references for only a few of the verses; youth must look them up to find out which verses they are. Examples of impostor verses include: "God helps those who help themselves." "God won't put more pain on you than you can bear." "Cleanliness is next to godliness."

Greeting Card

Guide youth to create a greeting card for a Bible character in crisis or joy. Suggest that the front be an illustration of the Bible passage, the inside be a paraphrase of the Bible truth taught in the passage, and include the signature a personal word of care.

Guided Paraphrase

Paraphrase means "to put into your own words." Rather than ask, "What does this passage mean to you?" let youth show you by paraphrasing the passage. When students paraphrase Scripture, they tell what it means to their lives at that time. This usually works best as an individual assignment, each youth writing his or her own paraphrase of the whole passage and then reading all or part of it to the class. When time is short, assign each youth one or two verses to paraphrase. Then read them in turn to create a class paraphrase.

Paraphrase can be used several ways by giving different instructions:

- *Simple paraphrase:* Write Romans 5:1–5 in your own words. Use words that someone who has never been to church would understand.
- *Paraphrase by circumstances:* Write Matthew 6:19–23 as you would live it at the mall.
- *Personalized paraphrase:* Write about yourself fighting a series of temptations as Jesus did (Matt. 4:1–11).

Variation: Write several one-line paraphrases of a verse, and instruct students to choose the one they believe best represents the application of that verse and why.

Haiku

A haiku is a poem form with a total of seventeen syllables, five in the first line, seven in the second, and five in the third. Guide youth to put the day's passage in haiku form. Sample:

Christianity
Makes the difference each day
'Cause I have a Guide

Hangman

Challenge students to secretly pick a key phrase from the passage or summarize the verse in one word. Then guide them to write spaces for each letter of their phrase or word on the chalkboard. Challenge the others to guess the phrase or word, letter by letter. For each mistaken letter draw a part of the hanging man. The initial goal is to guess the word or phrase before the man gets drawn. The ultimate goal is to enable students both to teach and memorize Bible passages.

Hats

Guide youth to create hats that communicate the truth of the Bible passage you are studying. Provide large paper, markers, and scissors. If only small paper is available, make miniature hats.

Variations: Let the hats show a Bible character's personality, communicate a role Christians are to play as believers, or picture each youth's favorite Bible verse.

Headline

Guide students to write a headline for the Bible passage you're studying. This summarizes the passage, reminds students that Bible events actually happened, and shows how to apply that passage to real life.

House Map

Guide students to draw a map of their house and to label each area with an action, sentence, or attitude they could do in that room to obey the Bible passage. Sample instructions:

- Draw a floor plan and include five things in your house that matter to you. Read Matthew 6:33 and add to your blueprint ways Jesus would guide the use of each of these items. How does putting Jesus first change the value of these items?
- How does 1 Corinthians 13:4–7 impact how you act in each room of your house?
- What do people in your family do that bugs you in each room of your house? How will you keep from doing those same bugging actions back, according to Luke 10:27?

- If Jesus drew a blueprint of the way he wanted you to behave in your house, what would be on it?

Idea Chains

Challenge two or more teams to each make a strip of ideas longer than the other teams. Give each team a stack of small paper, masking tape, and a marker. Direct teams to write on each paper one idea that meets the assignment. Guide them to tape the papers end to end to make a longer list than the other team(s). Youth love the competitive nature of this type of listing. Sample assignments:

- Name ways you can witness at school.
- Name specific ways to love your neighbor as yourself.
- Name ways to wait until marriage for sex.
- Name sins youth commit.
- Name temptations youth face.
- Name ways to resist temptation.
- Name actions you can do to make this group more loving.
- Describe characteristics of a perfect date.

Variation: Each idea must begin with the last letter of the previous. Example: Witness with word**s** . . . **S**how faith with my actio**n** . . . **N**eed people.

Variation: Create an actual chain by using strips of paper and looping them together after an idea is written on each.

Letters

Pass out stationery and invite youth to write letters to apply the Bible passage. Ideas for letters include the following:

- *To Jesus*: Write a letter to Jesus talking with him about how you will live the Bible command we're studying.
- *To a Bible character*: Write a letter to someone in the Bible asking for advice on a specific part of the passage. Example, to the apostle Paul. "You recorded in 1 Corinthians 13:5 that love is not easily angered. I get furious with my boyfriend. Does this mean we aren't in love?" Exchange letters and answer as the Bible character might answer.
- *From a Bible character*: Write a letter from the viewpoint of one of the characters in the passage telling what happened, why you think it happened, and how your life is different because of it. Example: You are Leah and you know your dad is planning to marry you off to someone who is in love with your sister (Gen. 29:16–30).

- *To a friend:* Write a letter to your friend to thank him or her for living a Bible command. (Examples of such commands: Practice reconciliation, show forgiveness, tell about Jesus).

Letter Maze

Guide students to draw the Bible verse or summary in maze form: rather than write the letters to the words in a straight line like usual, close up the spaces and write the letters in all directions. "Be quick to listen, slow to speak" might be written like this:

```
        I S T E    O W T O S P
  B        L     N S L      E     5 1 1 9
  E Q U I    O              A     E
      C K T                 K J A M
```

License Plate

In many states you can pay an extra fee to order a custom-designed license plate. Purchasers use any combination of seven letters and spaces to show their identity or make a statement. Examples: A hearing aid dispenser uses EARS4U; a cocky high school senior might express his seniority with BOW-DOWN. Guide students to compose a seven-letter-and-space license plate to show the way to express the passage you've studied that day. A student eager to live Ephesians 5:15–16 would use SEIZDAY for "Seize the Day." That same senior who wants to remind herself that God has absolute seniority might put IFALSRT (pronounced "I Fall Short") for Romans 3:23.

Discuss with these questions: "Why is this identity worth paying extra for in terms of commitment, dedication, time? What dividends does it pay?"

Limerick

A limerick is a poem form with two long lines that rhyme, followed by two short lines that rhyme, followed by a final long line that rhymes with the first two long lines. Limericks can express Bible themes or introduce students to one another (or to you). To write a limerick, guide students to list the characteristics of the Bible theme or person and then arrange them in limerick form. This example introduced a dear friend who raises roses and teaches a girls' Sunday school class:

> There once was a woman named Josie.
> Who said she would brag on her roses.

But they had a black spot,
So she decided to not,
And instead teaches girls about Moses.

Listening Sheet

When you have a great amount of information to present in a short time, write key points from that information on paper. Leave key words blank so youth must listen to fill them in. Then as you lecture, the listening sheet makes hearing more interesting. The blanks cue youth on what facts to listen for. Writing on the listening sheet not only gets students involved; it increases their learning retention.

Maps with Meaning

Maps can spell b-o-r-e-d-o-m. Cultivate youth's interest in maps:
- Use maps that have personal meaning to students, such as maps of their classroom, school, home, or weekly routine. Sample: Guide students to draw every desk in a school classroom, mark their own desk, and name ways they can minister to the people in the other desks.
- Get youth involved with Bible maps by writing on them, tracing the path, filling in details, illustrating what happened in each location, and more.
- Cut the map into a puzzle, adding a piece each week.
- Reduce or enlarge the map.

Math Solution

Guide youth to write the Bible passage in mathematical form such as an equation or a math concept. Addition, subtraction, multiplication, division, and more can be used to show youth's discoveries in a Bible passage. Your math whizzes will have fun with this, and all youth can do well with it. Just give enough guidance. Examples:
- What two things in this passage add together to make God happy?
- For James, *Favoritism + You stand There = Judging with Evil Thoughts.* What verses tell about each action?
- What's your friendship quotient?
- What proofs in this passage show that God really does care for you?

Missing Letter Alphabets

To settle in students' minds a single word or a short phrase, print a series of alphabets with a letter missing from each. Youth find the missing letter in each line to spell the key word or phrase. Even better, let youth prepare these alphabets on their computers and bring them to class. Say, "Pick a word or verse you want the rest of us to remember from this week's passage. Then type for each letter an alphabet with that letter missing. The easiest way to do this is to type a full alphabet, copy and paste it, and then remove the letter for each line. Bring it Sunday for each of us to solve." The key word might be the Bible passage for the day, the memory verse reference, or a word from that passage. For numbers use lines of one through ten and leave out a number to be found and written. Here's one for James 1:22:

_   ABCDEFGHIKLMNOPQRSTUVWXYZ

_   BCDEFGHIJKLMNOPQRSTUVWXYZ

_   ABCDEFGHIJKLNOPQRSTUVWXYZ

_   ABCDFGHIJKLMNOPQRSTUVWXYZ

_   ABCDEFGHIJKLMNOPQRTUVWXYZ

_   234567890

_   134567890

_   134567890

New Verse to a Poem

Choose a familiar poem such as "Roses are Red" and direct each youth to add a new verse that communicates the truth of the Bible passage you're studying. The familiar meter helps youth feel comfortable adding a new verse. Stress that youth include at least three phrases from the Bible passage you're studying. **New Verse to a Hymn** in chapter 10 guides a similar process in music form.

90- Second Assignment

Lay large assignment sheets along the edges of the room, using as many sheets as you want groups. Explain with great anticipation that, on your cue, youth will run to the paper they choose and fill it with dozens of ways to fulfill that assignment. Say that they will have 90 seconds to fill the paper, that they are to come up with more ideas than any other group, and that only four members can join each group. Build eagerness to move. Then say GO! This rapid listing method guides youth to work quickly and with interest. If your theme is reaching out, and you want three groups, your assignment sheets might say: Ways to reach out with the telephone; Ways to reach out in person; Ways to reach out on-line.

Pass Notes

Youth love to pass notes between classes. Put this practice to great use by directing youth to write notes as part of their Bible study. This helps students communicate to each other what they see in the Bible passage. Give instructions on what to write and to whom to pass the notes. Encourage youth to write just as they would to a friend at school. Once the notes are written and passed, the holder reads it aloud. Sample instructions:

- If you were one of Daniel's friends in the fiery furnace, what note would you pass to your friend the next day? Find the details in Daniel 3:8–30. Be sure to include what got you into the furnace in the first place, the scary parts, and the happy ending. Pass your note to the person two seats over from you.
- How would you have felt the next day after you and your brothers threw Joseph into the pit and then changed your mind and sold him? Write a note telling what happened and how you feel about it. Find the details in Genesis 37:17–28. Pass your note to the person on your left.

Poetry for Everyone

Poetry can express Bible truth in a way that is clear and easy to remember. It can communicate security, assurance, oneness with Christ, and other crucial faith foundations. Provide a poetry format, such as the one below, so students who do not usually write poetry can succeed. Suggest that students feel free to use a format other than the one you offer. Forms include **Haiku**, **Limerick**, and **Write a New Verse to a Poem**, all described in this chapter. Another form is the topic poem. Here's how to do it:

_____
(Write the theme word such as "Resurrection")

_____ _____
(Write two adjectives that describe the theme word)

_____ _____ _____
(Write three verbs that describe how to live the theme word)

_____ _____ _____ _____
(Write a four-word phrase describing the effect of the theme word)

_____
(Write a word that means the same as the theme)

Sample of a finished poem:

Resurrection

Amazing Freeing

Obey Smile Triumph

Fear death no more

Life

Prescription

Distribute a mock prescription form that you've made by writing "Rx" on small, white paper. Direct students to write a prescription for solving a certain problem or preventing a spiritual illness. Choose the problem or illness based on the passage you are studying. Examples:

- Write a prescription for solving conflicts according to Matthew 18:15–20. Include the expected results and the side effects.
- Write a prescription for preventing foolishness using two proverbs in Proverbs 14. Include the expected results and what to do about certain side effects.

Profile Story

Guide students to write a story about how a teenager lived or could live the Bible passage you're studying. Urge them to keep these fiction, knowing that much real-life truth will be taught in them. Fiction keeps students from bragging on themselves or elevating some peers to superspiritual status by writing about them. Fiction also allows students to combine the best of several testimonies.

Recipe

Distribute recipe cards, and invite students to tell you the Bible's recipe for living a Bible principle like holiness. Guide each student to list at least three ingredients and tell how to blend and bake those ingredients. In the ingredient listing or the cooking instructions, insist that students quote at least twice from the Bible passage(s) you're studying that day. Sample assignments:

- Write a recipe for spirituality according to Galatians 6:1–10.
- Write the recipe for acceptable speech according to Ephesians 4:29, telling how to use the two ingredients.
- Write the recipe for joy according to Philippians 1. Include at least six ingredients.

Adaptation: Guide some students to write a recipe for talking, some for listening, and some for another aspect of communication. Show how the recipes together make a complete meal. Adapt for other themes.

Report Card for Self

"Do you live the Christian life?" This question cannot be answered yes or no. So to keep from asking yes/no questions when you want students to look at how well they are doing, guide youth to create a report card for themselves. Topics that work well with report cards include Fruits of the Spirit (Gal. 5:22–23), the Ten Commandments (Exod. 20:1–17), New Life/Old Life (Col. 3), and the Sermon on the Mount (Matt. 5–7). After giving themselves a grade on each aspect, suggest that youth include comments at the bottom on how God wants them to improve on their failures and keep growing their strengths.

Variation: Instruct youth to leave their ungraded report cards in their chairs with their names at the top. Direct each classmate to find and mark one quality on each card to which they could give an A. Then let youth continue marking themselves.

Variation: Guide youth to grade themselves on undesirable qualities such as acts of the sinful nature (Gal. 5:19–21). In this case F's are great!

Variation: Give grades to TV shows, movies, and magazines.

Report Card for Teacher

Periodically (perhaps at school report card time) let your students evaluate you. Give each a report card and invite them to give you letter grades with pluses and minuses just like at school. Encourage comments. (See sample on following page.)

Stickers

Invite youth to write their responses on stickers. Create stickers with adhesive paper available in school supply catalogs or by cutting standard white name tags. Or let students cut the stickers in the shape that communicates their assignment. Sample assignments:
- According to this Bible passage, what actions produce friendships that really stick together?
- Create a symbol, sign, or face that communicates this Bible passage.
- Summarize this Bible passage in one phrase on your sticker.

Sunday School Teacher Report Card

_____   Makes the Bible clear

_____   Gives me a chance to discover answers for myself

_____   Shows how faith applies to everyday life

_____   Uses words I understand

_____   Helps me correct mistakes without making me feel dumb

_____   Gives good advice

_____   Keeps class interesting

_____   Shows Christlike actions and attitudes

_____   Demonstrates love for me and other youth

My favorite part about class: _____

What I'd most like changed: _____

Comments _____

_____

_____

Students can put the stickers on their Bibles, school notebooks, anywhere they choose.

Tags For Clothing

Give students paper cut in the shape of clothing tags. Explain that clothing tags tell what the clothing is made of as well as how to care for it. Direct them to find in the passage several actions or attitudes that Christians are to be made of and what care will keep these elements strong. While studying the beatitudes in Matthew 5, a student might write, "Because my beloved grandmother died last month, I'm about 60 percent mourning combined with 40 percent hungering and thirsting for righteousness. I'll allow myself to be cared for by comforting friends but won't get self-centered about it. I'll care for righteousness by reaching out to my mourning sister." Students don't have to use percentages and can simply list elements instead.

Variation: While studying passages about money and stewardship, guide students to create price tags for items youth buy. Discuss when money is an accurate measure of worth and when we need other measures of worth.

Variation: Create price tags for activities, the tags telling how much of each day should be spent there. For example, school needs at least ten hours—eight at school and two of homework—yielding about 42 percent of the day; sleep needs about eight hours yielding about 33 percent, and this still leaves me 35 percent to do fun stuff and to eat. Stress honoring God by doing all twenty-four hours well.

Telephone Numbers

Guide students to remember the location of a Bible passage or the truth of that passage by putting it in phone number form. Like regular phone numbers, words or letters can be used. Let your students' creativity run wild. All they need is seven letters, numbers, or syllables. Or they could include an area code for a ten-digit number. Samples:

- Real power available at PHI-L413 (Phil. 4:13)
- Learn how to love by dialing 1-John4V728 (1 John 4:7–8)
- When you feel far from God, Call unto him: 2Chron7–1416. (2 Chron. 7:14–16)

Thermometer

If students are grading a single characteristic such as a forgiving attitude, willingness to obey God, or toleration of fellow believers, guide them to draw a thermometer and give themselves a temperature. Let them decide their own "degree marks." Perhaps they would divide the thermometer into fourths, the top fourth labeled "Decisively obeys God"; the next fourth, "Usually obeys God"; the third fourth, "Wants to obey but lets other concerns push God out"; and the bottom fourth, "Usually ignores God except when at church retreats." Students could mark themselves at various degree marks within each quadrant. For some characteristics they might include fever levels that are too high or danger levels that are too low.

Tombstone/Epitaph

Guide youth to create a tombstone with an epitaph for a Bible character, letting at least one line be a quote from the day's passage. Suggest about four lines for the epitaph. An epitaph is the writing on the tombstone that summarizes the person's life. Epitaphs can also be written in longer form as obituaries.

Variation: Guide youth to write epitaphs for themselves, each writing what he or she wants to be remembered for. Let these help in setting life goals for the next week, month, year, and decade.

Tribute

Explain that a tribute is a way to remember someone in a meaningful way. Guide youth to write a tribute for a Bible character, quoting at least twice from the passage you're studying. Ways to give tribute include writing memoirs, composing a poem, creating a scrapbook, or naming a way you'll be different because you've known this person.

Variation: Guide youth to write the tribute they want people to give to them, and then name a plan for living that kind of life.

T-shirt Motto

Distribute paper that has been cut in T-shirt shapes, or use actual T-shirts and fabric markers. Direct students to put in their own words a T-shirt motto that demonstrates the passage you are studying. Urge them to write it so it would make sense to a nonbeliever as well as encourage a believer. Instruct students to add a logo, design, or symbol that matches the saying. If you use cloth T-shirts, encourage students to wear them. If you use paper, display them in your Bible study room, or let youth take them home for their rooms.

Adaptation: Create with the students a T-shirt motto and logo with computer software and print it on T-shirt transfer paper, which is available in office supply stores and some department stores. Then attach the logo to T-shirts.

Want Ad

Guide students to define characteristics or qualities of Christianity with a want ad. Give each student paper, sample want ads, and pencils. Here are some sample instructions:

- Write an ad for a faithful believer based on Hebrews 11.
- Write an ad for a Christian who acts the same at school and church. Base it on James 1–2. Explain why hypocrisy won't work in this job.
- Write an ad for a prophet based on the Book of Amos (or whatever character you are studying).

Why God Says So

Guide students to compete in two or more teams to list reasons God's rules make sense. First direct the teams to list the reasons *not to* obey the rule. Then direct the teams to list reasons *to* obey the rule. Your goal is to prompt youth to list more reasons *to obey* than *not to obey*. Senior highers generated these lists:

Why should we wait until marriage to have sex?

1. God says so.
2. Can get sexually transmitted diseases.
3. Virginity is a great wedding present.

4. Makes marriage more special.

5. I'd be jealous if my spouse had already had sex.

6. Can die from AIDS.

7. I'd feel better about myself.

8. People respect you more, including the one you marry.

9. I'll wish I hadn't if I do it.

10. Virginity is something to be proud of.

11. Marriage is a great place to learn how to do sex.

12. Kids cost money, and I don't have much.

13. Kids and marriage are a big responsibility.

14. When I talk to people who aren't virgins I say, "Any day I could become like you, but you can never become like me."

Why should I have sex before marriage?

1. It feels good.

2. I have trouble waiting.

3. I can't get a date any other way.

4. I don't want to be called frigid.

Because youth listed so many more reasons to obey God, they themselves demonstrated the wisdom of God's ways. If the *not to* list is longer, point out the weakness of human reasoning. Then invite youth to generate more reasons *to* obey God. Finally, in testimony to God's power, highlight the power of God's reasons even if they are fewer in number.

Word Bubbles

Rather than give students paper with a question at the top, enclose the question in a word bubble and leave a blank word bubble for the answer. It looks like a cartoon. This simple variation encourages less stained-glass language and more real-life talk.

Adaptation: Use other interesting writing spaces like the "glass" of a magnifying glass or the brain of a thinking Christian.

Plus . . .

Try these other ways to use paper to study Scripture:

• Add to, illustrate, or create from scratch a Bible time line.

• Make a mobile with symbols or illustrations from the Bible passage.

• Test students before the study (grade privately; focus youth on what they need to know).

• Test students after the study (congratulate them on what they learned).

- Have them write a response to a question that they don't have to sign (privacy encourages honesty).
- Involve students in making transparencies of the Bible truths for an overhead projector.
- Make bookmarks with Bible verses or paraphrases.
- Write essays about how you will live the Bible passage.
- Write a litany (responsive prayer, often with repeating response).
- Write on bandages ways to help people who are hurting.
- Find the mistakes in pictures by comparing them to Bible truth.
- Create multipage maps to guide you to your destination. Each page includes a small portion of the trip, places to eat, places to refuel. Sample destinations include "Ability to Do a Quiet Time Each Day" and "Temper Control."
- Use optical illusions that make students think of a Bible truth.
- Outline the Bible passage or Bible book.
- Write a biography about the Bible characters you study.
- Create Bible placemats to remind youth of a particular truth.
- Create and spend fake money (use in a study of stewardship).
- Graph how actions impact the result to show why God's ways work.
- Change one letter per word to study a series of words related to your passage or a series of passages. Samples for David include: cling, sling, slink, and so on.
- Use washable markers to create a temporary tattoo that shows commitment to obeying a certain passage.
- Label drawings with word bubble stickers. Photography shops and department stores carry them.

Chapter 8

꒰꒦꒱

Talk Starters

The one who talks is the one who learns

Rationale: Teenagers love to talk. Even quiet kids will talk when they feel treasured and listened to. As your students talk, they solidify their beliefs and understand their faith. As your students voice their ideas in light of the Bible, they have opportunity to evaluate those ideas to see how well they really work. As your students share their personal experiences with friends, problems, and activities, they discover that the Bible is the true source of better friendships, solved problems, and fun activities. As your students talk about the Bible, the Bible becomes a comfortable friend and a way to listen to God. The methods in this chapter help these powerful discoveries happen.

Teaching Tip: What teenagers say is not always what they believe. As you lead discussions, realize that talking is a way to try on ideas and to discover whether the ideas are true. Rather than act shocked, guide youth to think through their ideas with Bible facts and God's guidance. As youth do their own talking, they discover that God's ways really do work. Let youth do more talking than you do so they can develop a strong faith based on firm study of the Bible.

Teaching Tip: Encourage youth to talk by finding something in every response that you agree with. Even totally wrong answers can be welcomed with "I see how you drew your conclusions—let's find out more about that." When youth's answers and experiences are treasured, they venture living the truth. When you care about youth, they feel God must care.

Teaching Tip: Youth talk when they feel safe and smart. Enhance this by introducing these rules in your group, emphasizing the reason for each:

1. When someone talks, listen and understand.
2. No laughing at or ridiculing what anyone says or feels.
3. When you disagree, do so agreeably.

4. When someone makes a mistake, affirm your love.

5. On "everybody participates" questions, each person gives an answer.

Agree/Disagree

Many Bible truths are like diamonds: they show the truth from many facets. To bring out these facets, guide your students to talk with one another in a walking discussion called Agree/Disagree. Post four signs:

Agree   Disagree   Strongly Agree   Strongly Disagree

Direct youth to stand and come to the middle of the room. Read a statement about the Bible passage that gives the students an opportunity to demonstrate the truth from all sides. Point out the signs, and instruct youth to move to the sign that tells how they feel about the statement (some signs will attract several students; other signs will attract few). These samples aid the discussion of Matthew 6:5–8:

- Praying in public is mostly for show (based on vv. 5–6)
- Private prayer is the best way to talk to and understand God (based on v. 6).
- Short prayers are better than long ones (based on v. 7).
- Even though God knows what we need, we should state what we need anyway (based on v. 8).

Ask members of each group to explain their choices, beginning with the smallest group to affirm their courage to stand alone. After talking with all four groups, show how each comment brings out some aspect of God's truth.

Bring youth back to the center and repeat the activity with the next statement.

Because students actually walk from position to position, they think through the ideas while walking and watching others walk. Then they know that at any moment they may be called on to express an insight, so they pay closer attention. Make certain you call on someone different each time and at random to give everyone at least one opportunity to express an insight. Prompt reluctant talkers by good-naturedly reminding them that everyone will talk at least once. Removing the chairs takes away the temptation to sit down.

Ball in the Hand

To keep all youth from talking at once, introduce a rule that only the one holding the ball can speak. Then pass a fun-to-hold ball. It will take a while to get into the habit of talking only when holding the ball, but this builds a listen-to-show-you-value-the-speaker habit. This is even more valuable to hearing-impaired members who read lips and must know who's getting ready to speak.

Compare to Today

Guide youth to compare the Bible passage to something that happens today. Example: "If there was a hole in the girls' bathroom at camp, should you look? What would David say about this after his experience with Bathsheba?" (2 Sam. 11:2–12:13). Comparison helps youth notice how and why Bible truths work yesterday, today, and tomorrow.

Competition

Youth will do almost anything with more vigor if they are competing against another team. Use competition positively rather than for putting down the loser. Let your teams be no larger than about four to ensure everyone's participation. Ideas to compete over:
- Name more reasons to obey God than any other team.
- Name more things to praise God for than the other team.
- List more ways to show love to a friend than any other team.
- Name more things you like about the other team.

Fake Answers

While studying cults or common misunderstandings, give youth some fake answers that are exposed by the Bible passage you're studying. Challenge them to prove you wrong with specific verses in the passage. Examples: The fake answer "Jesus was just a good man" can be answered with Hebrews 1:3–4. The fake answer "It doesn't matter what you believe as long as you're sincere" can be answered with 2 Timothy 2:15–16. The fake answer "It's OK because we're in love" can be answered with Jeremiah 17:9.

Favorite Word

Provide several words or phrases that describe or summarize the Bible passage. Invite youth to choose their favorite and tell why. Their whys frequently bring out unique insights.

Finish the Sentence

This process guides youth to express how the Bible passage applies to their lives. Post sentence fragments that will prompt expression about your passage. Samples:

- This passage makes me want to . . .
- It would be hard to obey this passage because . . .
- It would be easy to obey this passage because . . .
- I think God wants me to change . . .
- I think God is proud that I . . .
- I most admire [name of Bible character] in this passage because . . .

Four Words, Two Words, One Word

Invite your students to summarize the truth of the Bible passage in four words. Then guide them to summarize it in two. Finally, invite them to name the one word that helps them remember how to live the Bible passage.

Variation: Ask the first few youth to use four words, the next few two words, and the last few one word.

Variation: Assign a different word in the passage to each youth, and challenge them to find it and tell why it is important to the passage.

Gossip

One of church people's greatest sins is gossip—repeating the dirt they hear about other people. Some have learned the advantage of good gossip—repeating only true and positive things about people. Turn both into a positive teaching approach by inviting your students to gossip about the Bible passage. "What would people have been saying about this event?" "What dirt would they have spread?" "What good would they have rejoiced about?" "How would God have wanted the people to respond to both the negative gossip and positive words?" This motivates students to read the passage to find the tidbits of news for the grapevine. In the process they learn the facts of the passage. They also learn how to respond to people who say or do ugly things. Example:

> I think people might have spread rumors about Mary's pregnancy. Some might think she and Joseph had not waited for marriage. We don't know what she said to people who may have said ugly things about her, but we do know she honored God by marrying Joseph and waiting until after Jesus was born to consummate their marriage. Maybe she talked to a friend about how much the gossip hurt her. Then she went on and developed a good attitude anyway. Even if no one else believed it, she knew the child was conceived by the Holy Spirit.

Harmony

God is not a God of confusion. Help youth sort through their confusion about Bible passages by guiding them to see how seemingly opposite passages actually harmonize with each other to present the whole truth. Examples: "Why did James say 'Faith without deeds is dead' (James 2:26), and Paul emphasize 'Righteousness that comes by faith' (Rom. 4:13)?"

Intentions

As you encounter Bible characters in your study, encourage youth to evaluate why they think the characters did and said what they did: "What do you think her intentions were?" "What do you think he thought would happen and why?" "What actually did happen?" "Why did intentions matter or not matter?" This process guides youth to discover that there is more to a decision than good intentions. As youth study Bible characters' decisions, they can avoid their mistakes and imitate their successes.

I Wish

I Wish is a form of sentence completion that encourages youth to pinpoint areas in themselves or in their world that they want to change. The Scripture becomes the source of answers, methods, and plans for change. Students discover which wishes God wants them to embrace. Use "I wish . . ." to start a session or to begin a discussion on how to apply the Bible passage.

Begin with a fill-in-the-blank sentence. Write the sentence on paper or the chalkboard to help youth focus on their answer rather than remembering the sentence. Choose a sample like these, and then challenge students to find verses in your passage to help them fulfill their wishes:

- I wish I could stop before I give in to the temptation of _____.
- I wish I could recognize the destructiveness of words like _____ before I say them.
- I wish I could overcome my worry about _____.
- I wish my home was more _____.
- I wish I was more _____.

Lecture Limit

There are times when you need to present a concise amount of information to your students. So humorously call it Lecture #36 or #41, and invite your students to time you. Limit these minilectures to about ninety seconds. You can say an enormous amount of information in that time. Because students know the time is limited, they'll be more attentive.

Letter Demo

As students enter, give them each an official-looking letter on official stationery that gets them ready to receive the truth of the passage you will study. Watch for reactions, and discreetly jot down comments to share later. Call for discussion prompted by the letter. This sample prompted youth to see why the Bible's plan for giving is a great one:

> Dear Church Member:
>
> Your share of the expenses of the ministry and upkeep of _____ Church is $380.95 per year. This may be paid in one lump sum, or it may be divided into fifty-two (52) equal payments of $7.32. These payments are due beginning January 1, 2000.
>
> If the first month's payments are not received by February 1, you will be summoned to appear before the Stewardship Committee to explain your willful neglect of your God-given obligation. See 2 Corinthians 8:1–12.
>
> [Signed by the pastor]

Guide youth to write "VOID" across the letters and collect them. Follow with questions like these: "What is your first reaction to this letter?" "What does this Bible passage recommend as a better way to motivate giving?" (or whatever your theme) "Why should we give through the church?" "What should we do when people refuse to give through the church?" "When they take more than they give?"

Life Deck

Prepare a deck of life cards, writing one of these life areas on each card:

- school
- church
- friendship
- playing sports

- family
- home
- dating
- watching sports

- free time
- magazines
- money
- with someone I like

- books
- clothes
- television
- with someone I don't like

Use the life cards in one of these options:

- *Option #1*: Display the cards upside down and direct each student to choose one. Invite them to apply the Bible principle that you're studying with a **30-Second Speech** (see below).

- *Option #2*: Challenge youth to arrange the life area cards in a certain order. They might order them from easiest to hardest to do, from the place God wants the most emphasis to the least, or what they understand best. Example: "Where is it easier to forgive? At school or home? In what area does Jesus want you to focus your talking time? your praying time? your understanding time? How do you understand God's plan for your free time?"

- O*ption #3*: Guide youth to give themselves a grade on how well they live for God in each life area, specifically as it relates to the Bible theme.

- *Option #4*: Make a deck of cards specifically related to your theme. If you are studying how Jesus responded to suffering, make a deck listing illnesses and crises. Ask, "What practical action does Jesus want you to take to help someone during this pain? What should you say and not say? do and not do?"

Like Me

Guide youth to tell how they are like or not like a Bible character. This helps them decide how to imitate that character or avoid that character's mistakes. Post a pair of questions like these examples, and direct each youth to complete them:

- I am like Adam/Eve because . . .
- But I am not like Adam/Eve because . . .

Variation: Guide youth to tell how they both live and don't live according to a Bible principle. Example:

- I live forgiveness [or whatever your Bible theme] when I _____ because . . .
- I neglect forgiveness [or whatever your Bible theme] when I _____ because . . .

As youth discuss, frequently insert the truth that Christianity is more like a journey than an instant bestowal of perfection (Phil. 3:12). We daily struggle to be more Christlike in our actions and attitudes.

Like/Unlike

Guide youth to understand Bible concepts and characters by describing them. Post these sentence fragments, and guide each youth to complete them:

- God [or heaven, or whatever your theme] is like ___ because . . .
- God [or heaven, or whatever your theme] is not like ___ because . . .

Answer samples:

- God's love is like a blanket because he makes me feel cozy, but he is not like a blanket because he really can keep the bad guys away at night.
- Heaven is like home because I will feel happy there, but it is not like home because no fire or robber can hurt it.
- Forgiveness is like freedom because it brings back a relationship, but it is not like freedom because not everybody wants it.

Object Talk

Object lessons can make Bible truth clear and memorable. Guide youth to do their own object lessons by placing in the center of the table several objects or pictures that relate to the passage you are studying. Invite youth to choose one, and use it to explain the Bible passage. Provide student-book commentary and other resources. For Luke 15 you might present a toy lamb, a coin, a picture of a boy, a picture of a dad, a picture of a big brother, a toy pig, a robe, a ring, sandals, and a toy calf.

Variation: Let youth create their own object lessons from something they brought with them in a billfold or purse.

Opposite Understood

To help youth discover how to obey God, guide them to verbalize ways to disobey him. To guide youth to discover why they should obey God, direct them to see how disobeying God brings pain and sadness. For things the Bible tells them not to do, prompt youth to tell what to do instead. As youth find the opposites they see the reason for God's prohibitions and the yes behind God's every no.

These opposite examples from Colossians 3:5 show what yes to put in place of the no:

The opposite of . . .	is . . .
sexual immorality	being loyal to my marriage partner even before I'm married
impurity	being true myself and demanding purity of others
lust	seeing people as precious people, not objects
evil desires	wanting the best for people
greed	generosity
idolatry	keeping God in first place and in command

These do's from Colossians 3:12 list sad things that happen when we don't obey God:

The opposite of . . .	is . . .
compassion	using people
kindness	ignoring how my actions impact people; hurting feelings
humility	know-it-all-ness
gentleness	brutality
patience	anxiety, worry

Discuss with questions like these: "How can doing the opposite of what God forbids bring happiness? Why does sadness always result from failing to do what God promotes? How have you seen this sadness or happiness?"

Variation: Direct youth to rewrite the Ten Commandments without "no" or "not." One of my favorites, written by a high school junior for "Thou shalt not commit adultery," was, "Do it with your spouse, and keep it in your house."

Panel Discussion

Enlist two to four people whom youth respect to serve on a panel. Good panel discussions are short, involve the audience heavily, and use people who are more interested in answering questions than in making speeches. To increase the success of your panel:

- *Use topics that are already interesting to youth.* Examples: A panel of guys and girls talk about what guys like in girls and vice versa; a panel of teachers suggest how to please teachers; a panel of kids and parents explain how to make a happy home.
- *Write a few audience participation questions to get discussion rolling.* Subtly distribute these among the students.
- *Use the panel early on in class time.* The panel can continue if interest is high or you can move on to other things when interest wanes. Recognize that the personality of the group that day heavily influences a panel.

Paper Plate Feelings

Instead of just asking "How do you feel when you are lonely?" give youth paper plates and pencils. Direct them to write on the outside how they look to other people when they are lonely and to write on the inside how they look to themselves. As youth show and talk about the plates, they answer the question. It takes a little longer than just asking, but the quality of response is deeper and touches the heart rather than the surface. Use this technique with any feeling that matches your Bible passage: fear, excitement, worry, anger, infatuation, love, confession, forgiveness, grief, repentance, and more.

Parable Telling

Jesus used everyday objects and experiences to explain spiritual truths—we call them parables. After studying one of Jesus' parables, invite youth to use an everyday object to tell their own parable about the theme. These examples were generated by a group of tenth grade boys studying Matthew 13:18–52 and Mark 4:1–34:

- Sin is like pizza. It tastes great at first, then it's bad (indigestion).
- The kingdom of heaven is like a self-sealing bag—you have to let Jesus help you seal out bad actions and attitudes or you'll get spoilage in your life.
- Sin is like an ink pen—it works at first but when it's empty you have nothing.
- The kingdom of heaven is like an apple orchard—there are bad apples among the good for a while.
- Sin is like a spider web—you're attracted to its sparkle but get all trapped in it and the sticky feeling stays a long time.

Phrase Names

Guide youth to give the Bible characters phrase names similar to the way some Native Americans might have done. John the Baptist might be called "Locust-Eater" and "Unafraid-Teacher." Esther might be called "Approaches Boldly" and "Advocate for Her People." Let these names help youth remember how the Bible person served God, and how youth today might imitate them.

Adaptation: Let youth give these names to each other based on a single Scripture passage. Names from Philippians 2 might include "Does-Nothing-out-of-Selfish-Ambition" and "Looks-to-the-Interests-of-Others."

Adaptation: Let youth choose names for themselves based on a single Scripture passage, letting a name become their goal for spiritual growth that month. See the first adaptation for examples.

Prayer Processes

Prayer is talking with God. But many students feel uncomfortable praying aloud. So let your students practice prayer during class in a variety of ways. Rather than limit prayer to the end or beginning, pray at different times of the study. Also, continually communicate that prayer involves both talking and listening to God. Consider the following prayer formats:

- *Popcorn prayer*: Students pop in a sentence whenever they choose. Check them off mentally to wait for everyone to pray. Let students know ahead of time that you'll wait for them. This provides both a comfort and a push to participate.

- *Amen after prayer requests and praises*: Explain that when youth share prayer requests and praises they pray an open-eyed prayer to God. After this they don't have to repeat them all, but simply say "amen." Enlist one student to write prayer requests and praises as the rest of the group shares them. Enlist a second student to call on class members who raise their hand to share a request or praise. Enlist a third to say "Amen" after all requests and praises are shared. This involves three youth each week in the prayer guiding process.

- *Prayer Tag:* Call on the youth with the birthday closest to today to pray for someone in the group. That person is "tagged" and prays for someone else. Continue until all have been tagged once. The final person prays for the orginal. Repeat if time allows.

- *Celebration*: Rather than just voice requests, guide each student to share at least one good thing that has happened that week as a praise to God. Consider letting some prayer times be all praises.

- *Listening*: Because prayer includes listening, guide students to write one prayer entirely from God to them. Enforce silence for this. Allow volunteers to read all or parts of their listening prayers.

- *Pause*: Wherever a need or joy is shared, stop right then to pray about it. Let these prayers be about a sentence long and voiced by a different teenager each time.

- *Notes to God*: Because many students find it easier to write notes than to talk, guide them to write a note to God. Let volunteers read them aloud.

- *Prayer in the hat*: Guide students to write prayer requests on papers and place them in a hat or box. Take turns drawing from the hat and praying a sentence for that need. This allows the anonymity that encourages honesty. Discourage trying to identify handwriting.

- *Partners*: Guide students to pray in partners, sharing concerns and then praying for each other's concerns. Caution the partners to treat each other's requests with tenderness.

- *Prayer chain*: Wherever needs arise during the week, each student calls another until all are praying. If any student is not at home, or an answering machine takes the call, the caller phones the next student on the list to keep the chain going. The last one on the list is you, the teacher, to confirm that the chain has made it all around the class. If an hour after starting the chain you hear nothing, call down the list to jump-start it where it stopped.

- *Prayer recipes*: To help youth know what to say, give a form or acrostic. A form sample is: (1) Say HI to God; (2) Say WHY you like following him; (3) Tell about a GUY (or girl) in your life you want help relating to—friend, family, or romance; (4) Ask whether the PIE of your day is divided up the way God wants it to be; (5) SIGH in the comfort of God's continuing love. This acrostic spells A.C.T.S., which stands for—**A**doration, **C**onfession, **T**hanksgiving, **S**upplication (requests).

Props

Use a telephone for talking to God or for giving advice to a friend. Use squares of toilet paper for naming ways to clean up the messes in our lives. Use any item that helps youth focus on the truth of the Bible passage. How might you use these props to make your Bible lesson clearer?

• facial tissues	• paper cups	• timer	• paper towel
• clock	• clay	• set of keys	• nail
• plant	• money	• light bulb	• bread

Prove Me Wrong

Play "devil's advocate" and challenge youth to prove you wrong with truths from the Bible. This is particularly effective on truths youth resist. When youth have to do the convincing rather than the bucking, they tend to convince themselves. Here are some ideas:

- Prompt conviction to take a vow of abstinence with "Prove me wrong that it's OK to take a drink or two at a party as long as I don't get drunk."
- Prompt conviction to obey God with "Prove me wrong that God won't mind if I sin once in a while."
- Prompt conviction for the truth of the Resurrection with "Prove me wrong that Jesus didn't really rise from the dead."

Playing devil's advocate also works well to guide youth to disprove wrong statements like these:

- Obeying Christ takes away all your fun.
- Becoming a Christian means I have to give up too much.
- Jesus doesn't know what life is like today.
- Jesus wouldn't accept me after what I've done.
- God's will is always opposite to my hopes, dreams, and plans.

Rather This or This?

To help students think through their options ahead of time, give two options to ponder. This enables youth to see the positive and negative results of each, and they can choose God's best on purpose. Examples: "Would you rather struggle through persecution for a little while or suffer in hell forever?" "Would you rather ignore a friend or refuse popularity?" "Would you want tons of money or tons of wisdom?" "Would you rather fight a disease or a disability?" After a few starter "rathers," let youth name the "rathers" since they know what they currently struggle with.

Road Signs

Display pictures of road signs. Invite each youth to choose one and use it in a sentence to tell how to live the Bible principle you are studying. Road sign possibilities include Bump, Stop, Crossing, Yield, Speed Limit, Buckle Up, Do Not Enter, Slippery, Caution, Hospital, Sharp Curve, Deer Crossing, Danger, Detour, Slow, Reduce Speed, No U Turn, Airport, One Way, Road Closed. Use these sample starter questions to guide youth to answer with road signs:

- How have you used Jesus' temptation-resisting principles from Matthew 4?
- How would you have responded to the serpent in the Garden?
- What advice from this passage would you give someone who is about to enter high school?

Variation: Make a set of road signs for each youth. Read a passage such as the Ten Commandments (Exod. 20), Colossians 3, or James 1. Invite youth to hold up signs during the reading to tell how they have responded to that phrase.

Sin Is . . .

Rather than tell youth what to do and not do, guide them to verbalize a definition of sin so they can recognize it and refuse it for themselves. Sin is more than a list of wrongs; it's an attitude toward God and people. For example a smile sounds like a loving thing, but when it's a smirk, it betrays—and betrayal is a stinging sin. Point your students to specific Bible passages to help them recognize and refuse sin. Follow the same process for other Bible concepts like mercy, obedience, temptation, and more.

Something I Like/Something I Don't Like

To enhance youth's discernment skills and help them take steps toward solidifying their beliefs, guide them to share something they like and don't like about a viewpoint or statement. Youth are experts on their own opinions, so they start talking; in the process they refine their opinions and bring them in line with Scripture. Also, saying a like with every dislike keeps youth from growing too critical. Finally it helps them evaluate without automatic acceptance or rejection.

Use "Something I Like/Something I Don't Like" for evaluating statements like these:

- If you're a Christian, God will bless you with money and health.
- Suffering is part of the Christian life.
- Praising God makes everything better.

Adaptation: When evaluating Scripture itself, change the assignment to "Something I find easy to obey/Something I find difficult to obey." We don't want to debate Scripture.

Something Right/Something Wrong

When studying temptation, cults, spiritual deception, or other themes with half-truths, invite youth to spot something right and something wrong with specific statements or actions. This heightens youth's discernment of falsehood, while acknowledging the appeal of many half-truths. Explain that half-truths are one of the strongest tools Satan uses.

Here are some sample statements to evaluate with Something Right/Something Wrong: "It's OK to do wrong once in awhile because you can be forgiven" or "I'm the only one who will be hurt by this, so I can do it."

Variation: Challenge youth to evaluate their magazines, TV shows, or music with Something Right/Something Wrong.

So What?

Youth ask this question all the time. So ask "So what?" during Bible study to prompt youth to tell you why a Bible truth works in real life. The answer to this question is where the water of faith hits life.

Spiritual Everything

Teenagers who go to church and answer questions in class frequently think they are perfectly spiritual. Many see no conflict with saying ugly words in the church hall or acting aloof at school. Avoid this tragedy by regularly focusing on how to be spiritual. Spirituality is not going to church all the time and talking in a holy sounding voice. Being spiritual means letting God guide each aspect of life—even the way you argue or the way you do your homework. The Bible says it like this: "Whether you eat or drink or whatever you do, do it all for the glory of God" (1 Cor. 10:31). Here are just two ways to focus on spirituality:

1. During the application portion of each Bible lesson, invite students to express how to be spiritual in that circumstance—how to let God guide.

2. Hold an entire lesson on spirituality. Challenge students to take turns naming any issue, particularly focusing on ones that don't seem to be spiritual issues. As they name candidates, guide classmates to tell how that issue is a spiritual one and ways to honor God through it. Examples:

   • Issue: Playing cards

     Response: Playing cards is a spiritual issue because when I play the wrong card, I could respond in a way that honors God ("That's OK, everyone plays a wrong card sometimes"), or I could slander God by slandering you ("How stupid! Why did I ever agree to be your partner?")

   • Issue: Burping

     Response: Burping is a spiritual issue because I'm unspiritual when I draw attention to myself by burping. I'm very spiritual if when you burp accidentally I keep you from feeling dumb by saying, "No problem, I know you didn't mean it."

   • Issue: Clothing

     Response: I can dishonor God by wearing clothes that are too short or too low or too tight. These make other people think of sex rather than see me as a person. Or I could wear clothes that make me feel both comfortable and rightly attractive. Then I can forget myself to care for others. Third, I can avoid clothes that make an angry statement or support greedy companies.

Spiritual Impact

Rather than just define spiritual principles—such as Holy Spirit conviction, sin, guilt, repentance, reconciliation, sanctification, transformation, righteousness, and more—guide your students to describe how these spiritual principles impact everyday life. These five questions help youth recognize the impact of spiritual principles:

1. What does it look like?
2. What does it act like?
3. How do you know it when you see it?
4. What should you do when it comes?
5. What happens if you ignore it?

Adaptation: Many students don't want to deal directly with sin and guilt or invite God's sanctification and transformation. Invite students to break down these hesitancies with questions like "Why do we hesitate to get rid of guilt? What makes us fear righteousness? How can we treasure righteousness? What are the advantages of responding to rather than ignoring guilt?"

Spirituality with Silence

Agree that talking about faith doesn't mean someone really has faith or lives faithfully. Allow youth to name some hypocritical actions they've seen without naming people or identifying details. Ask, "Why do your actions matter?" Guide youth to name ways they could show with their actions that Jesus really does make a difference. Consider these ideas:

- smile with care
- listen with real compassion
- defend a person who's being attacked/slammed
- befriend both new and established folks
- fold towels and do other chores without complaint or calling attention to self
- bow your head and say blessing at school lunch table
- cut words like "So!" and actions like snubbing

Talk Differently

While *never* doing this in a way that makes fun of the way someone talks, guide students to speak in unusual ways to make a point. For example, guide students to read James 3:5–6 while holding the tips of their tongues, to show the impact the tiny tongue has. Then proceed to talk about ways to tame the tongue and why it's worthwhile to do so.

Or talk with only churchese, words that only those in church would understand. Then direct your students to translate as you study the Bible passage.

10-Second Testimony

Invite students to talk for ten to thirty seconds about how a specific Bible principle has influenced their lives. Ten seconds is long enough to say something significant but short enough not to scare. It equalizes talking by prompting all to participate and allowing none to overtalk. Good-naturedly interrupt at the 10-second point (fudge a little if a shy student has just gotten going). Here are some topics for which 10-second testimonies work well:

- Tell about a time the Holy Spirit convicted you.
- What sin keeps coming back to haunt you?
- How have you changed an action because of guilt?
- How has God led you to choose the righteous action when another action would initially have been easier? How was righteousness best in the long run?
- What action or attitude shows that the retreat changed your everyday life?
- Tell about something neat you've learned during a sermon.

Adaptation: Some students may have more to say after the first round. Allow another ten seconds until everyone who wants a second turn has one. Then allow more turns until all have said as much as they want. But keep the talk in 10-second intervals—this equalizes talking and assures that no one monopolizes the sharing.

30-Second Speeches

Explain that everyone will talk for thirty seconds on a topic that relates to the day's Bible study. For the Beatitudes, your topics might be *poor in Spirit, mourn, meek, hunger and thirst for righteousness, merciful, pure in heart, peacemakers, persecuted because of righteousness* (see **Life Deck** above for one-word application topics). Write the speech topics on cards and invite students to choose one. Let students choose without looking by fanning the cards in your hand. Or lay the topics out and let students choose their favorite. Point out sources of ideas such as the Bible passage, personal experience, or the student book. Call on volunteers until all have spoken.

Adaptation: Use speeches for opening when you want kids to focus on a need or question the Bible passage can meet. Use them for closing when you want kids to think about applying the Bible passage.

Top Ten

Guide students to write the Top Ten for whatever your Bible passage. While studying the last eleven chapters of Genesis, students might articulate the "Top Ten Ways Joseph Chose to Do Right No Matter What the Circumstances." While studying Revelation they might share the "Top Ten Reasons I Will Stay Loyal to Jesus until the End." Name the number one reason last.

What If?

Ask: "What if ___?" to help students think through how they'd manage tough situations before they get into them. This reminds youth that even the most unexpected thing can happen to them and that God will always help them figure out what to do. Guide students to think through dilemmas they may face with these steps:

1. Together list all the worries the group has by calling them out spontaneously. Call these "what ifs" (What if my mom dies? What if I fail geometry?). As youth hear other students list worries, they'll discover that the only bad worry is the one we choose not to solve.
2. Divide the "what ifs" among the group, and challenge them to list for each "what if" at least three things a teenager could do about it, especially as guided by the Bible passage(s) you're studying.
3. Discuss the solutions. Suggest ways you might prevent some of the problems and how to cope with the ones you can't prevent. Point out that knowing what we would do can give some relief from worry. Using verses like Philippians 4:13 assure youth that God will get us through every "what if."

Word Association

Challenge students to write the first word that comes to their mind when they hear a theme word. Get the association process rolling with neutral words like *girl* (*boy*) and *young* (*old*). Then give Bible words like *regret* or *reconciliation*. Invite students to share what they wrote and why. Affirm a wide variety of responses, pointing out how each comment helps us understand the topic. Then open to the Bible passage to discover even more understanding.

Yarn Toss

This familiar technique is new to many of today's students. Those who are familiar with it still find it appealing: they know it means honest discussion on a topic that's important to them. Seat the group in one large circle. Hold a ball of yarn. Explain that only the person holding the yarn can speak and that after speaking the holder wraps the yarn twice around her wrist and then tosses it across the circle to another student.

To begin, introduce the question or topic and briefly give your answer or comment. Wrap one end and toss it to a student across the circle. That student now speaks on the topic, wraps yarn, and tosses the ball to another student. Continue until everyone has spoken. Then invite any who have something else to say to raise their hand. Toss to them. These are examples of themes that work well with yarn sharing:

- How I have grown in Christ as a result of these Bible studies.
- What I like about our group.
- One thing I could do to make our group more Christlike.
- How the Ten Commandments/Sermon on the Mount impact my life.
- How you have helped me grow in Christ this year. (For this one, have students toss the ball to someone who doesn't already have the yarn wrapped around his wrist and tell them how they help them).

Use the web that forms in the circle to generate further discussion:

- How do our daily lives show this kind of connectedness to people?
- What does the yarn in the middle teach us about our topic?
- How is our group like what we see in the middle of the circle?
- How do we affect people by the way we handle our hold on the yarn?
- How will you yank or not yank on people daily?

Yes . . . But

Quicker than debate, this talk format encourages students to look on both sides of a multifaceted issue so they can see how God wants them to respond. Explain that both the "yes" and the "but" statements must be absolutely true. Example: "Jesus is Lord of all" . . . but "many people refuse to obey Him." Then discuss how we Christians can make certain we obey him daily rather than just give him lip service.

Plus . . .

Here are more ways to talk about Bible passages:

- Create analogies, similes, and metaphors.
- Retell the Bible events in your own words.
- Present book reports or article reports.
- Have the group give a lecture, each speaking, each adding discoveries.

- Have students give each other pep talks (Heb. 10:24–25 in action).
- Guide the entire group to bombard each member with compliments (see **Affirmation by Name, Affirmation by Secret Compliment,** and **Spiritual Gift Saying** in chapter 12).
- Say what you want your obituary to read and how to make it so (see **Tombstone/ Epitaph** in chapter 7).
- Choose from a potpourri of words the one(s) that best expresses truth.
- Form listening teams (as you lecture, each listens for something specific).
- Engage in problem solving (list options, evaluate, choose the best).
- Use chapter 9 **Predicament Cubes** to discuss rather than act solutions.

Chapter 9

❧❧

Art and Drama

*Artistic expression encourages the involvement that
produces learning.*

Rationale: Artistic expression invites involvement. When fingers move to
draw, doodle, or dabble, minds concentrate on spiritual truth. When bodies
dramatize Bible events, youth understand what Bible characters went through
and how God wants them to respond as a result. When you study the Bible
through art, learning occurs in several ways:

- The artist remembers what she or he created.
- The observer remembers the presentation because sight, sound, and
  movement are involved. The more senses students use, the more they
  remember.
- Students can take home a physical reminder of the Bible study, or the
  experience of drama.

You may be a teacher (like me) who shies away from art. Overcome your
hesitation for the sake of Bible learning. Each time you venture teaching the
Bible with art, notice the deep spiritual insight your students present. To
introduce a study on Jesus' view of divorce, I gave my senior high students a
lump of play clay and instructed them to shape what divorce feels like. Rand,
usually very well behaved, threw his against the wall. Very upset, I said,
"What are you doing?" Evenly, he replied, "You feel smashed against the
wall when your parents announce their divorce." He was right. And I've
never forgotten that truth.

Teaching Tip: When giving an art assignment, explain that the content of
the art is much more important than the finished product. Don't stifle your
artistic students by saying art doesn't matter. But don't let pressure to produce a polished work inhibit your less artistic students from expressing their
ideas.

Teaching Tip: Instruct youth to focus on a particular passage of the Bible as they do their art and drama. This keeps them from pulling out old learning like "Jesus loves me" and "Be nice." Students instead make new Bible discoveries and express them beautifully.

Teaching Tip: Good Bible study methods aren't the active or fun stuff that comes before or after the Bible study. They are the Bible study itself.

Add a Face

As youth read the Bible passage, direct them to pencil simple faces next to each event. These smiley, frowny, confused, or afraid faces could tell how the character in the story is feeling, could tell how God feels about the character's actions, or tell how the event impacts youth's lives.

Adaptation: Invite an artistic youth to draw sample faces and make these into stickers for the class to use. Rather than sticker their Bibles, show students how to slip a paper under the page and put the stickers on the page.

Book Jacket

After a Bible book study, guide youth to make a book jacket that invites teenagers to read that Bible book. Let making the book jacket guide students to review what they discovered. Include these elements:

- Illustrate an event from the Bible book for the front cover.
- Write back cover copy with at least three quotes from the Bible book.
- Pick an excerpt from the Bible book that will make readers want to read the rest. Write this inside the front cover.

Remind students to address the book cover to students who know little or nothing about the Bible. Provide paper in various colors, scissors, markers, and more.

Cartoon Drawing

Challenge students to draw a cartoon that illustrates the Bible events or applies the truth taught in those verses. Cartoon drawings will range from simple to complex in the same class—that's perfectly fine. Each is equally valuable because of the ideas expressed. Do praise those with detailed drawings just as you would a youth who expresses words well, but highlight something wise in *every* cartoon. Possible cartoon assignments:

- Draw the exodus in cartoon form, according to Exodus 13:17–14:31.
- Illustrate how to do one of Ephesians 4:25–32 "live in the light" commands. Use two or more cartoon frames.

- Read the case study, and draw how you think God would advise you to solve it based on this Bible passage.

Charades

Guide youth to act out, without words or sounds, biblical actions or attitudes as guided by that day's Bible passage. Underline these actions and attitudes in your passage; then write one to a card with the verse reference. Remember not to pull actions from the entire Bible, but to focus on a single passage so youth digest it thoroughly. If you're studying 1 Corinthians 13, students could act out actions that are loving or not loving. If studying Revelation 1–3, students could act out good and bad qualities of the seven churches.

Clay Shaping

Give each youth a lump of play clay and direct them to shape it into the theme of your Bible passage. Shaping works especially well with hard-to-put-into-words terms like *faith, sanctification, justification, fellowship, hope*, and more. This method takes repeated encouragement but is well worth it. Just keep asking these three questions: "What does it look like?" "What does it act like?" "How do you know it when you see it?" When youth have all shaped their clay, invite each to share what it means. Highlight a spiritual insight in each.

Youth will stun you with their incredible spiritual insight. For example, when asked to shape faith, a teenager sculpted a brain. He said, "Faith is a decision to do what God wants you to do. That decision starts in your head and then commands the rest of you to act."

Adaptation: Let students keep their clay throughout the session to squish and mold. This absorbs energy and helps students focus on the discussion. The conditions for keeping the clay are not throwing or passing the clay, and the clay must stay in one piece. Use play clay because it doesn't rub off on hands, clothes, or the church building. The wilder the colors the better youth tend to like it.

Collage

A collage is a collection of pictures, words, or objects attached to a surface to demonstrate a Bible truth or theme. These items include both flat objects like magazine pictures, and three-dimensional objects like fabric, small objects, pipe cleaners, and more. A **Montage** (see below) has only the flat objects. The beauty of collage and montage is their use of several items to communicate a single truth. The danger is that youth get carried away reading the magazines or newspapers you provide. Overcome this by tearing out and bringing key pages, or by limiting time so youth have to work quickly. Here are some effective themes for collages and montages:

- Sin in the world
- Good in the world
- Places God's attention is needed
- How the world could be if we all lived like God wants us to

Coat of Arms

Guide youth to create a coat of arms for the Bible person or family in your passage. Many coats of arms have about four sections, are shaped like a shield, and have a banner-like slogan across the top. Sample assignments for each section:

1. In one section illustrate what this person said about God.
2. In a second section illustrate an action or attitude that showed this person loved God.
3. In a third section illustrate a mistake or discovery this character made.
4. In a fourth section illustrate what you will do as a result of knowing this Bible person.
5. In the banner across the top, write the slogan God would choose for this person.

Comic Completion

Cut the word bubbles out of Sunday comic strips, and back the blank spaces with white paper. Direct youth to fill in new conversations and actions that illustrate how to live out the truth in the Bible passage. Use comics strips that are several weeks old, or students may remember the original words. Also, allow students to add more word bubbles and characters.

Adaptation: These take a long time to make. To reuse them, cover with contact plastic before youth write on them. Then let youth write on the plastic with erasable markers.

Computer Screen

Guide youth to draw a computer screen that shows how to live the passage you're studying. This drawing could include words to say in the word processing screen or spreadsheet, icons that show what to do when, toolbars with resources to draw on, and more.

Bonus: If you have a laptop computer, bring it along to give sample screen layouts.

Dialogue

A dialogue is a conversation between two people. You could combine two characters from the passage, or a present-day youth with a Bible character. Form pairs of youth using one of the team-forming methods in chapter 16. Direct each pair to write a dialogue based on the Bible passage you are studying. Stress that they stay closely tied to the Bible, quoting as much of the Bible passage as they can in their dialogue. It's OK for all students to do the same passage because the dialogues will vary widely, each bringing out a measure of truth. Or divide a long passage, giving each duo a section to dialogue.

Variation: Guide youth to write dialogues between themselves and God, or between a Bible person and God.

Doodle Sheet

If students doodle while you're teaching, they will remember what you say. Provide doodling paper and instruct your students to doodle on it every truth or insight they hear. Award a point for each doodle, or a group hug to the one who finds the most doodles with verse references next to them. Provide creative borders or idea starters around the edges of the paper you provide. Your border might even be a quote from the Bible passage. Enlist your most avid doodlers to create these borders in advance.

Variation: Cover the table with white paper to create a group doodle sheet. Encourage youth to fill the table by the time the study is over.

Dramatize

Drama is not just for the hams and the dramatic. In fact, you'll be surprised at the youth who excel at drama. Because students are actually in the Bible scenes, they remember what they said and did. Drama occurs any time students act out a passage. These options can help you include drama in your Bible study:

- **Bible as Script** (see details in chapter 4)
- Present Bible events as they would occur today. Have youth compose a contemporary skit that closely parallels the parable or other Bible pas-

sage you are studying. Suggest that students include a section from each verse.

- Dramatize a new ending to the passage—what would have happened if this person had not obeyed God? What would have happened if they did obey God?
- See **Role Play**, **Tableau**, and other drama options in this chapter.

Draw Anytime

Whenever you assign writing to your students, offer the option to draw the response. Many youth pack more into a picture than words can say.

Draw the Passage

Assign each youth one or more verses from the passage you are studying, and instruct them to illustrate those verses. Because visual images can be easier to remember than word ones, drawing can provide powerful learning. Youth more readily see Jesus as Protector after they have drawn sheep in a pen protected from a wolf (John 10:1–15).

Ways to draw are endless: Youth might fill the wall with a mural of the scenes in the Bible passage, replace each Bible word with a picture (see **Rebus**, chapter 13), represent the truth as a political cartoon, do a comic strip, use stick figures, use fancy figures, use color, use black and white, and more.

Adaptation: Rather than draw the Bible passage itself, guide youth to illustrate how to live the Bible passage in their own lives.

Finish the Doodle

Provide students with a beginning doodle, perhaps a shape or squiggle. Challenge them to complete it so it shows the truth of the Bible passage. Or invite youth to make beginning doodles and pass them to the left. Or invite each to make a beginning doodle to collect and use during a later session. Duplicate and use one of these doodles a week until they are used up.

Graffiti

Graffiti are words and symbols that express reaction to a given theme. Give your students their own markers, and direct them to draw or write on huge paper their reactions to a passage as you read it aloud. Drape this paper across the table or on the wall. For maximum learning and greatest comfort, prompt all to draw at the same time rather than watch what the others draw. Discuss the graffiti wall with questions like these: "Why did we react this way? Which of these reactions should we let God change? Which express what God wants?"

Jigsaw Puzzle Picture

Guide youth to create jigsaw puzzles that demonstrate the Bible passage you're studying. Then send the pieces home as remembrances of the study. Here are some different ways to do this:

- When studying the body of Christ, obtain a huge piece of heavy paper or cardboard (perhaps a refrigerator box), and guide youth to cut it into the number of youth present. Give each youth a piece to reassemble the puzzle. Then give each youth a marker to draw on the puzzle answers to questions such as, "Why is each person important according to the passage we're studying? What does the person on your left contribute to this group? on your right?"
- Create a puzzle that demonstrates how God wants the pieces of our lives to fit together. This can be done as an individual or group project. Discuss with this question, "How are our lives to be an interlocking whole rather than a bunch of pieces?"
- Create a puzzle that shows steps to solving problems. Discuss with these questions, "How does God help us puzzle out problems? How are problems solved one piece at a time? What pieces might keep us from getting into messes again?"

Logo

Guide youth to create a logo to communicate your Bible passage. Suggest they think about clothing brand logos, contemporary Christian music band logos, and other logos to recognize elements that make logos communicate. Caution youth not to copy any logo but to create a fresh one. Call on each student to explain his or her logo, quoting from your passage at least once. This combines talking and drawing to provide complete learning.

Masks

Guide each student to create a mask that illustrates a Bible character's virtue (or vice) or the truth taught in the Bible passage you're studying. Then let them act out that virtue or truth using the mask. Masks can be as simple as paper and marker or as complex as a three-dimensional sculpture of papers, objects, and paints. Masks give a sense of anonymity that can free your students from inhibitions as they act.

Adaptation: Bring in masks to use during any drama. Choose ones that match the characters the students will be playing. Again notice how comfortably youth dramatize with a mask on.

Mime the Passage

To pantomime is to dramatize with no words or sound. Because actions frequently speak more powerfully than words, guide students to mime the truth in your Bible passage. Students have to study and understand the passage before they can effectively act it out. So this procedure works well as a closing step or a second-to-last step. Suggest students choose actions that will prompt observers to think about what the passage says and how to live the passage in present life. Form at least two mime teams, each miming for the other while the observing team follows along in their Bibles.

Monologue

A monologue is a drama with one person. Guide each youth to write and perform a monologue based on the day's Bible passage. This could be a presentation of the Bible character's experiences and feelings, speaking to God and repeating back what God says in the passage, and more. Suggest each student limit his or her monologue to sixty seconds to allow time for everyone to speak.

Adaptation: Talk about times we let our prayer become a monologue, and discover ways to make it a dialogue.

Montage

A montage is a collection of pictures and words that communicate a Bible passage or Bible theme. It differs from **Collage** in that all the items are flat. Use it like **Collage** above, except use only paper objects like photos, illustrations, and magazine cutouts.

Mural

This drawing option makes it easy for youth to absorb long and dramatic passages like those in the Old Testament. A mural is several scenes in consecutive order. Begin by displaying a large sheet of paper on the wall, floor, or table, and providing markers. Assign a portion of the long passage to each student, and direct them to illustrate that portion. For example, each teenager might draw a plague from Exodus 7–11.

Hint: Youth like these best when everyone works at once rather than one draw while the rest watch.

Name Tags

Let your name tags be part of the teaching process, as well as help you remember student names. You might pass out name tags preprinted with a verse you'll reference during the study. Or invite students to make their own name tag to motivate them to study, to examine the passage, or to apply the passage. Examples:

- To motivate youth to read the passage, give these instructions: "Tear your name tag into a symbol of this Bible passage." While studying Acts 18:1–4, a student might shape a house to remind him to invite people home to study like Priscilla and Aquila.
- To guide examination of the passage, give these instructions: "Make a name tag that shows a characteristic you think Jesus wants you to express." While studying Matthew 25:1–13, a student might shape an oil lamp to remind her to stay alert to everyday good she can do while waiting for Jesus to return.
- To guide application of the passage, give these instructions: "Tear your name tag to show how you will be like the Bible character in our study." While studying Matthew 3:1–12, a student might shape a locust to remind himself not to call attention to himself, imitating John the Baptist in that.

Paper Cup, Foil, Paper Clip, or Pipe Cleaner Shape

Use anything moldable for meaningful dabbling. Where possible let the material match your theme. For example: Bend paper clips into the personality Jesus wants to form in you. Shape foil into the attitude God wants you to show. Give instructions and encouragement similar to **Clay Shaping** above. Consider the following sample assignments for each material:

- *Paper Cups*: Shape how you felt the last time someone was sarcastic with you or criticized you. After all have shared, instruct students to pretend the person has apologized. Direct them to return their cups to original form. The cups will still have wrinkles or tears. Use this to illustrate how crucial it is to use words positively in the first place—some damage cannot be repaired (Eph. 4:29).
- *Paper Clips*: Invite students to list several sins. Direct them to choose one and shape the effect it has on the sinner or the one sinned against.

After all have shared, explain that all these sinners have sought and received forgiveness from God. Direct youth to return the paper clip to its original shape. Bends and gaps will remain. Ask, "Is it OK to sin since we can get forgiveness? Why is it better not to sin in the first place?" Supplement by explaining that the effects of sin remain and that God's laws are meant to prevent trouble, not take away fun (Rom. 6:1; Rom. 1:20–32; John 10:10).

- *Pipe Cleaners*: Shape a ring that shows how people will know you're a Christian. One youth might leave the "jewel" section of the ring straight to remember to stay on the straight and narrow; another might make the ring totally round to show unity among friends.

Paper Shape

Provide various colors, shapes, and textures of paper. Invite students to express Bible truth in ways like these:
- Choose a color of spirituality and tell why it shows spirituality according to this passage.
- Demonstrate the texture of spirituality according to this passage.
- Make a hat that demonstrates spirituality according to this passage.

Photo Response

Gather photographs, illustrations, or cartoons that relate to your theme. Display them, and invite youth to respond to them in one of these ways:
- What is this person feeling?
- How do you think this person would react to today's passage?
- What does this person need from Jesus? from you?
- How would you meet and make friends with this person?
- What advice would you give this person based on our passage?

The more specific the solutions for the "picture person," the better your students will be helped.

Adaptation: Let your students take the photographs or draw the pictures.

Picture Poems

Invite youth to arrange words in the shape of the Bible truth you're studying. Let the words describe the truth, and the arrangement of the words illustrate the truth. For crucifixion youth might draw something like this:

```
              t
              o

              H
  M y   s i n s   l e d
              s

              d
              e
              a
              t
              h
```

Poster Creation

Any time you add a visual, you enhance learning. So use posters frequently, guiding youth to make them or write on them. Refuse to limit posters to rectangles on the wall. Use various shapes and sizes. Display them on the ceiling, on the floor, in the doorway, even on the backs of students. Invite curiosity by covering some posters until time to use them. Use computers or hand lettering. Encourage cartoons, stick figures, words, and ideas of great variety. Point students to specific passages to guide their poster making. Let these possibilities get you started:

- Create a set of footprint posters, telling the steps to becoming a Christian.
- Create a series of posters on how not to behave, then a series on how to behave.
- Create a poster of a totally contemptible person. Then name how to love this person.
- Create a poster of a totally likeable person. Then name what this person could do to get a bad reputation.
- Use huge, letter-shaped posters to spell out the theme of your study.
- Write questions inside flip posters that your classmates must open to read (see **Walk and Read** in chapter 4).

Predicament Cubes

When your curriculum includes case studies or you want to discover how to apply a Bible principle to real life, create predicament cubes. Fold a six-sided figure or use a square box. Tape to each side of the box one predicament, case study, dilemma, or problem that relates to your Bible passage. Invite each student to roll the cube and dramatize a solution to whichever situation lands on top, quoting from the Bible passage at least once. This roller may call on any number of classmates to be a part of the drama.

Adaptation: For added interest, form and roll a second cube with reactions: *cooperative, defensive, angry, curious, accusatory, open*. Or let one cube be six reactions and the other be six possible reasons for the reaction. Roll the reaction cube, and then match it to a reason and explain why. For a witnessing study, the six reactions to your witness might be *anger, silence, questions, fear, argument*, and *acceptance*. Possible reasons could include these: *treated badly by a Christian, sad event happened that they think God caused, under conviction by the Holy Spirit, want to know more, fear of God, agreement*.

Adaptation: Leave one side blank and invite students to suggest a predicament from their own life that the Bible passage addresses, when they roll the blank side. Offer the option to roll again if youth would rather not share a personal situation.

Role Play

A role play is a spontaneous drama during which at least one student plays a role he does not live daily. Popular roles to play include a parent, an enemy, someone with whom a teen conflicts, a teacher, or the teen as an adult. Guide youth to let the Bible passage guide them in the way they play their roles. Invite interest in role plays by using them in formats that differ from simply reading dialogue:

- *Twice*: Guide youth to role play twice: once in a way that's easy but causes more trouble, and once in a way that may be hard but solves the problem.
- *Two parts*: Give roles to youth separately and then bring them together to spontaneously act out what they would do with no previous consultation. Example:

Role 1: You borrowed your sister's favorite sweater without asking and spilled chocolate ice cream on it. The stain won't come out.

Role 2: You look in your drawer for your favorite sweater and discover it missing. When you go looking for it, you discover your sister has borrowed and stained it.

- *World problems*: Expand role plays to major world problems such as hunger and war. Let youth play leaders who have power to change these problems. Encourage students to respond as they think God actually wants leaders to act, based on the passage.

- *Board game*: Write the role plays on cards, stack them, and use them along with a board game to add interest. After the role plays, guide students to discuss "What did I do? What should I have done? What will I do when this actually happens?"

Script Writing

Guide students to write and then present a drama, based on the Bible passage you are studying. The writing process guides them to dig deeply into a passage and to digest its meaning. Challenge students to quote at least three times from the passage in every script and to present what they think God had in mind for that passage.

Sunglasses Action

Keep pairs of plastic or paper sunglasses in your teaching materials. Students tend to feel safer behind a pair of fake glasses and will say or dramatize things they might never do without them. Notice the many things you can do with sunglasses:

- Direct all to wear their glasses and tell how they *look* beneath the surface for real needs, or *see* the need for encouraging words.
- Distribute dark glasses and ask questions that relate to your passage, such as "What are we blind to? What do we hide behind? When do we walk in darkness rather than light? How does Christianity change the way we *see* the world?"
- Give glasses and invite youth to read the Scripture with them on. Ask, "What truths do you see when you look at this passage with spiritual eyes?"
- Give plain paper glasses and invite students to decorate them to communicate the theme of the day: seeing the good in people, seeing people as Jesus does, looking for opportunities to demonstrate faith, seeing chances to witness.

Symbols

Challenge youth to translate a Bible phrase into symbols that will help them live it. If studying the healing at the pool of Bethesda, students might draw a stick figure lying down and sad-faced. After Jesus walks up, the stick man is standing and smiling. The truth drawn is, "In Jesus' power I can stand even with the most debilitating problem or illness." Other students might use actual sticks. Still another student might bring a "weeble," the toy that always rights itself, to show the same truth.

Tableau

A tableau is a human picture, a still drama. It can be one frame or a series of frames. A classic, single-frame tableau is a human nativity scene. Guide students to pose the Bible passage in tableau. Divide the passage into scenes, and assign one scene to each trio of youth. As youth pose scenes, the others name the verses they are posing. Do this open Bible so youth will read and digest the passage while they dramatize.

Tangram

A tangram is a square cut into seven shapes. The original tangram has two large triangles, three small triangles, a small square, and a trapezoid (see sketch below). Cut the square into these seven shapes, or give youth the freedom to cut their squares into any seven shapes. Instruct students to arrange those shapes in a way that demonstrates the truth of that day's Bible passage. Their arrangements might show a symbol of the truth, a person doing that truth, and more. Though this may sound like playing, it forces students to think through the truth and express it in concrete form.

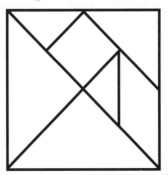

Treasure Map

Guide each youth to draw a treasure map showing the way to the treasure your Bible passage teaches about. Suggest they include landmarks to notice, pitfalls to avoid, and paths that lead to and away from the treasure you assign. Treasures could be a strong friendship, a good school life, a good guy/girl relationship, a happy family, or another treasure from the passage you're studying. Insist that the students quote from the Bible passage(s) you're studying at least twice on the map and include forks in the road that will lead to the right path or the wrong ones. The more specific their information, the better students will see how the Bible connects to life.

Vary the Drawing Tools

Youth who love to draw will be intrigued even further with a variety of drawing tools. Provide sticks and clay, charcoal and paper, marker board and dry-erase markers, colored pencils, fat markers, skinny markers, changeable markers, chalk and chalkboard—whatever is available and not too messy.

Word Pictures

Icebreakers and puzzle books abound with words arranged to communicate something different from what you first see. For example |R|E|A|D|I|N|G| stands for "reading between the lines," and PANT PANT stands for "a pair of pants." Guide students to put the Bible passage you're studying into a word picture. Perhaps the "joyful noise" in Psalm 100 might look like this: N☺ISE.

What If I Do/What If I Don't

Guide youth to act out their drama assignment twice. First guide them to dramatize what would happen if they disobey the Bible truth you are studying. Then repeat showing what will happen if they obey the Bible truth you are studying. Questions for discussion:

- Why does this Bible principle work?
- What problems do we create by ignoring God?
- How are God's commands always pointers toward happiness rather than prohibitors of fun?

Plus . . .

Explore these other options for teaching the Bible through art and drama:
- Experiment with photography.
- Show a clip of a movie to make a point.
- Interview someone who pretends to be a Bible character.
- Make before-and-after sketches on the difference Jesus makes.
- Present a comedy routine that communicates the theme of the passage.
- Make a flag that communicates the passage you're studying.
- Involve youth in dramatizing with puppets Bible events for younger viewers.
- Make a mobile with quotes from or applications of a passage.

- Evaluate films, videos, or filmstrips (see evaluation questions under **Music Bible Study** in chapter 10).
- Scratch off a sticker with a message underneath.
- Use gum wrapper chains to make bracelets or rings that remind youth to live a specific way for Christ.
- Draw a picture of (don't dye!) a hair tattoo that shows your commitment to Jesus.
- Prepare for and give a choral reading or speaking (see **Choral Speaking** in chapter 11 for details).
- Design a Zoetrope to show that our lives move with God at the center (a Zoetrope is a strip of pictures spun inside a ring to simulate movement).
- Use everyday items to create pictures of spiritual truth: squeeze all the toothpaste out of the tube and challenge the group to put it back in—compare this to words spoken or sins committed.
- Give a book review of a Bible book that will make listeners want to read and study it.

Chapter 10

꧁꧂

Music

*Music enhances Bible memory and
expresses Bible application.*

Rationale: Teenagers love music. Let your students' natural love for music motivate them to use it to study the Bible. The Bible says "make a joyful noise" not "create perfect music" (Ps. 100). So let joy, not musical talent, count when you teach the Bible with music. Music can enhance Bible memory, convey Bible moods, and make Bible application obvious. As youth sing, write, and evaluate, they remember, understand, and often experience Bible truth. Music also provides opportunity for musically talented youth to express Bible understanding in a way that is comfortable to them.

Teaching Tip: Choose songs that relate to the passage you're studying. Don't sing or listen to a song during or prior to a Bible study just because it's a fun or favorite song. The goal of music during Bible study is to learn that day's Bible passage or how it applies to life.

Teaching Tip: Provide a format for music assignments so youth know how to do it. Instead of saying, "Write a commercial on this Bible passage," guide youth to list current commercials, write the words to one, and then change the words to Bible verse portions (see **Commercial Creation** below). A set format makes the nonmusical comfortable and gives the musical freedom to expand.

Teaching Tip: One of Satan's favorite tricks is to spread the rumor that if music is loud it's bad, and if it's quiet it's good. Mellow music communicates some of the most dangerous lies. And loud beats don't drum up the devil—he's already plenty active. Prompt youth to evaluate the words, because those are what stay with them.

Affirmation of Faith Songs

Guide youth to write songs for one another. They can set these to a familiar tune or compose a tune of their own. Let each song be an affirmation of expressed faith, an encouragement to resist temptation, or an expression of confidence in their ability to handle the challenge ahead.

Form pairs and assign each pair to another pair. These pairs will write songs for each member of the other pair. Prompt the pairs to interview each other and then write two songs, one for each member of the other pair. Insist that each song quote at least once from the passage you're studying. Working in pairs ensures that two people affirm each person. Monitor the activity to keep all songs positive.

Character Theme Songs

Guide youth to write theme songs for the Bible character you are studying. Suggest they choose a commercial tune, a hymn tune, or a popular tune and change the words to become that character's theme song. Here are some sample characters and passages:

- Eve (Gen. 1:27, 2:20–25, 3:1–4:2)
- Enoch (Gen. 5:18–24; Heb. 11:5–6)
- Deborah (Judg. 4:4–5:15)
- Lazarus (Luke 16:19–31)
- Holy Spirit (Acts 2:1–4 and chaps. 14–16)
- Peter (Luke 22:54–62; John 21:15–24; Acts 2–4)
- Priscilla and Aquila (Acts 18:18–28)

Commercial Creation

Commercial writing is the perfect non–music lover's entry to using music to study the Bible. Youth compose brilliantly worded commercials that express Bible truth profoundly. Guide students to write in pairs, using these steps:

1. List as many commercials as you can. Fast-food places are classics.
2. Choose your favorite commercial, and write the words to the jingle with a blank line between each line.
3. Change the words syllable by syllable to tell how to live this Bible passage. Write these new words on the blank lines. (You must quote from the passage at least once).
4. Practice singing/saying/acting your commercial.
5. Sing/say/act your commercial when your turn comes.

Adaptation: In addition to using commercials to remember the passage, let your commercials advertise a specific something:

- Create a commercial that shows why Jesus' peace is superior to the peace the world offers (John 14:1–14).
- Write a commercial that shows how obeying God brings more freedom than living your own way (Rom. 7:15–8:2).
- Sell chastity: include why waiting until marriage is more loving. Use such passages as Genesis 2:23–25, Hebrews 13:4, and Proverbs 5:15–20.

Favorite Christian Songs

Hold a Bible study where all you do is play, sing, and appreciate each student's favorite Christian song. This has many benefits:

- Songs are a comfortable beginning point for youth to talk about God.
- Youth encourage one another by sharing how the Christian songs help them live their faith. They become the teachers.
- Youth learn that Christian music really can apply to everyday worries, can be of quality, and can be enjoyable.
- Youth discover ways that music can express their beliefs.

Invite all your students to bring their favorite Christian song with the words written on large paper. The song can be a hymn, a contemporary Christian song, or something they composed. Agree to bring a CD/tape player. Encourage those who compose their own songs to bring a guitar or the instrument they use. (They may bring a tape of themselves singing if that makes them more comfortable). Bring a few of your favorite songs to play if time remains.

Play each song, and encourage youth to sing along. Invite the one who brought the song to tell why he likes it, and invite others to add reasons why they like the song. Pepper the conversation by highlighting that Christian music can encourage us to trust God, to make smart choices, and to love our friends as we want to be loved. Compliment youth for their great music selections.

Hymn Evaluation

Guide students to evaluate how closely their favorite hymns match the Bible. Many hymnals include Scripture indexes at the back. Hymnals may also print the passage on which a hymn is based at the bottom of the hymn page.

1. Bring a hymnal for each student or pair of students.
2. Direct them to find a hymn that matches the Bible passage or theme you are studying.

3. Guide them to find at least one of the following:
   - A phrase that agrees with the Scripture
   - A phrase that disagrees with Scripture or could be worded better
   - A way to reword the wrong or poorly worded phrase
4. Sing the hymn together.

Lyric Sheet

To guide youth to listen closely to a song, distribute the lyrics with certain words missing. Challenge students to listen for and fill in the missing words. Choose the most important words to leave blank so the students will notice them. *Important*: Obey current copyright law. Often you can print lyrics for educational purposes.

Music Bible Study

A music Bible study differs from **Favorite Christian Songs** (above) because its goal is to evaluate music, not affirm favorites. To hold a music Bible study, invite all your students to bring a currently popular song (secular or sacred) with the words written out on large paper. Explain that together you'll sing and evaluate these songs. Agree to bring a CD/tape player. Bring several songs that are currently in the Top Ten to supplement.

Begin the Bible study by thanking God for music and the ability to distinguish between encouraging music and discouraging music. Then sing together the first song, directing youth to listen for phrases that agree with the Bible and phrases that disagree with the Bible. Provide paper to jot down discoveries. Point out that even music labeled "Christian" might teach things contrary to the Bible, and music labeled "secular" might have Bible truth in it. Encourage students to evaluate every song they hear, regardless of its label. Continue evaluating by asking questions like these:
   - What does this song teach about love? about life? about friendship? about people?
   - Where is it right about these according to the Bible? Where is it wrong?
   - If we did exactly as these words suggest, what would happen?
   - What is the song neglecting to tell us?
   - How does this song encourage your Christian life? frustrate its expression?
   - What solutions does the song suggest? How well would they work?
   - What words do you like?
   - What one line would you change if you wrote it?

- What overall grade would you give this song?

Variation: Use this process to evaluate movies, TV shows, magazines, and books.

Music Video

Guide students to make a music video based on your passage. It takes time but is worth it. Videos work especially well with tedious passages because the procedure motivates interest. Youth dig deeply in their Bibles for facts to make their songs interesting.

Music videos also tie a series of lessons together well: youth write lyrics as their application step each week and then film the lyrics as a set at the end of the unit of study. Steps to creating a music video:

1. Explain that youth will put the Scripture passage in song form. Direct youth to jot down points from the Bible passage for their song.
2. Guide youth to choose a song format and match the points from the passages to the music. Or simply write the lyrics in poem format and add background music later.
3. Videotape youth singing the songs.
4. Show the video. Note that youth learn four ways: finding Bible facts, setting them to music, singing the facts, and watching the facts. They remember forever the songs they write.

New Verse to a Hymn

Much of our understanding of God is based in the hymns we sing. Make your hymns even more meaningful by guiding youth to write new verses based on the Bible passage you're studying. **New Verse to a Poem** in chapter 7 guides a similar process in poetry form.

Report Card for Music

Rather than label music good or bad, invite students to give each song a grade. What grade would this song make for lyrics? Musical quality? True-to-life-ness? Ability to motivate right action and attitude? Let students choose their own categories or simply give an overall grade. Or read together Philippians 4:8 and invite students to give the song a report card with a grade for each of those categories.

Adaptation: **Music Bible Study** (above) is an expanded form of this evaluation process.

Singing Telegrams

Guide youth to create a singing message, complete with actions, that voices the truth of your passage. Ask them to name at least three people to whom they would want to deliver this message and why.

Song That Matches

You can't know every contemporary Christian song. But your students will. So invite their help in showing how contemporary Christian music can show how to apply the Bible to life. Weekly let a different student know your Bible study passage so he or she can bring a Christian song that relates to that passage. Ask that they write the words on a large poster so the group can sing along (check current copyright laws to make certain this educational use is currently legal). Play this song as youth enter. Then invite them to sing along at some point during your study. This might be used as a motivator, as a way to examine a specific verse in your passage, or as a closing challenge to live the passage.

Remember to include all youth by keeping a checklist that verifies you've invited everyone. Some may choose not to bring a song or may forget. Don't make a big deal of this. But keep rotating and keep asking every youth.

Adaptation: If you didn't plan ahead, distribute hymnals when youth arrive and challenge them to find a hymn on your theme.

Adaptation: Find a different hymn for every verse or section of your passage.

Song to Scripture

Pick a song that teaches your Bible passage. As students listen to the song, challenge them to open to that Bible passage and underline in their Bible phrases that match. Remember that most teenagers can listen to a song and read at the same time. Ask, "How does this song help us remember Scripture? How does it say to apply this Scripture?"

Why? to What?

Invite your students to teach you why they listen to music, and then choose music that best fits those reasons. Though the reasons tend to stay the same from generation to generation, youth want you to understand their generation. Once youth name their reasons, ask them how Christian music accomplishes each reason. This allows them to preach to you and overcome their resistance to Christian music. For example, many youth honestly believe that Christian music is not as good musically as secular music. Some isn't. But most is as good or better musically—it's just not on the radio.

Here are the typical reasons youth give for why they listen to music:

- the beat
- it gives voice to what they like or dislike
- imparts a feeling of freedom
- there's music to fit each emotion
- helps them concentrate
- has a calming effect
- has a stimulating effect
- it's something to do
- friends talk about the latest song
- music relates to issues they face
- singers are role models (so good Christian musicians can be great ones)

Adaptation: Guide your students to compete to name the most reasons to listen to Christian music. One youth said, "Listening to the words of Christian music is better than preaching."

Adaptation: Some Christian teenagers mistakenly believe that Christian music only sings about church and getting saved. Challenge youth to list the topics they like in music and then to find a Christian song that sings about it.

Plus . . .

These music methods give even more ideas for studying Scripture with music:

- Play a short segment of a Christian song and challenge youth to name it. This makes it popular to know Christian songs well. Choose ones that relate to your Bible passage.
- Speak a hymn rather than sing it.
- Work with the librarian to purchase Christian tapes for youth to check out.
- Study the content of the songs the choir will sing during worship.
- Sing a hymn or chorus that relates to your study.
- Use music comparison charts to find Christian music in the style your students like.
- With permission, sing in the choir for a week to discover how choir helps to lead worship.
- Wear Christian music T-shirts.
- Study Bible instruments and song styles.

- Memorize songs or memorize Scripture to music.
- Offer to trade a Christian tape for every secular one your students bring you.
- Write as many words as you can while listening to a song.
- Study the lifestyles of both Christian musicians and non-Christian musicians to choose whom to support and imitate.
- Ask why it matters what music we listen to, according to 1 Corinthians 15:33 and Hebrews 10:24–25.
- Encourage your students to watch Christian music videos rather than secular ones.
- Encourage students to sing as worship, both in church and at home.

Chapter 11

〰〰

Learning Projects

Guide students to present their learning to others

Rationale: Possibly the most reliable indicator of learning is being able to present that learning to someone else. A project enables students to do this. Projects provide triple learning:

1. Students learn while creating the project.
2. Students learn while presenting the project.
3. Students learn while watching other students present their projects.

Students can create projects independently or in teams of two or more. When students work together they build teamwork, experience success, feel part of a group, and become more comfortable about going to the Bible for answers.

Teaching Tip: To help your students bridge these kinds of friendships in their teams, form your teams in a different way each week. Ideas are detailed in chapter 16.

Teaching Tip: Remember that all youth are more alike than different. The teenager with Down's syndrome still worries about flirting, fashion, and being embarrassed by parents. The very school-smart teen worries about looking smart in spiritual matters. So treat your teenagers as a unified group, rather than segment them. Let their unique gifts blend to demonstrate the body of Jesus Christ.

Teaching Tip: Give specific and step-by-step instructions. The better students understand the process, the greater success they'll have with it. Also, they'll struggle less with "how" and can focus on "what" (the Bible).

Blessing

Especially precious for graduating seniors, group blessings can remind youth that they are surrounded by a cloud of witnesses who believe in them and know they can live their faith (Heb. 12:1). Call on students in a neutral order such as by the first letter of their middle names. Write the first student's name on the front of a card with a blessing verse such as Philippians 1:6 or Colossians 2:5. Then invite members of the group to name out loud blessings or hopes they have for this student. Write these on the card as they are listed, assuring that each card has about the same number of blessings. Add your own blessing to the card. Repeat for every student. Give the students their card as reminders that the group loves and believes in them.

Big Brother/Big Sister

Seventh graders eagerly enter the youth group, but once they get in they frequently feel lonely. Help both seventh graders and older members get to know one another by matching an older youth with each entering student. Expand the good of this process by matching all students with someone in a different grade. Then each time you study a passage, ask, "How can we as brothers and sisters live this passage?" Each younger student will learn ways to encourage his or her big sibling, and each older student will learn ways to encourage his or her younger sibling. To involve every youth every year, make different matches annually. Here is one way to structure Big Brother/ Big Sister:

- Match every incoming student with one already there. Ask for volunteers to miss no one, but feel free to privately invite those who may hesitate to volunteer.
- Match every other student with someone not in his or her grade. Make an effort to match school district, spiritual gift, and so on.
- Monthly, guide students to encourage one another in a specific way and during a meeting. For example, hold an incoming party during which matched students stay together the whole evening. The next month write encouraging letters to each other during your meeting—collect and mail them all. The next month brag on each other giving each other three specific compliments.

Adaptation: Guide your students to create and implement their own welcoming system, complete with matching method, checkpoints, and a fun name.

Choral Speaking

Guide your group to speak the Bible passage and its application with a speaking chorus that includes all students present. Similar to a singing chorus, this process talks "in parts": there are solos, group parts, unison parts, and whatever combinations the students determine is the best way to speak the truth. Encourage students to design their choral speaking with rhythm, surprise, and a variety of ways to vocalize.

Comic Book

Guide youth to work independently or in teams to create a comic book that illustrates the Bible passage you are studying. The comic books can be as simple as a sheet of paper folded in half to make four pages, or as complex as a sewn book. Suggest that the students follow this sequence:

1. Write one main truth you want to communicate from this Bible passage we're studying, and think about story lines that would communicate it.
2. Choose a way to live that truth and an advantage that results.
3. Choose a way to ignore that truth and a disadvantage that results.
4. Create one or more characters.
5. Show the characters ignoring and obeying the truth in a true-to-life story that makes the reader want to obey the truth.

Concordance Study

One of the most powerful ways to understand the Bible is to let the Bible teach about the Bible. When youth encounter a confusing Bible word, guide them to do concordance work—reading the word in several different Bible verses. Each verse helps students understand a little more of what the Bible word means because each verse provides context clues. Explain that a complete Bible concordance is a listing of all Bible words and the verses in which they appear. Each concordance is based on a particular translation. Some are in book form; others are on CD-ROM. Here's how to use one:

1. Choose a Bible word that you want to understand; pick one from the passage we're studying today.
2. Look up the word in the Bible concordance, and jot down all the verse references.
3. Read each verse listed that uses that word, jotting down what you learn from each verse.
4. Summarize your understanding of the word, based on your discoveries in the Bible. Tell specifically what it means in the passage we're studying today.
5. Share your discoveries with the class.

Each student can look up the same word or become an expert on a single word. While studying Romans 5:1–5, youth might do concordance work on words like *justified, faith, peace, Lord, grace, hope, glory, suffering, perseverance, character, love, Holy Spirit.*

Because concordance work is like research, some students will resist it. Others will gobble it up. Add a race element or a scavenger hunt flavor to add to its appeal.

Variation: Point out that some Bibles have only partial concordance listings in the back. These will give a few verses in the Bible where the word is used, but, though they are helpful, they may omit entries critical to your understanding of the Word.

Variation: Explain that many people use concordances to find a verse that they remember hearing but don't remember where it is. For example, look up *needs* or *riches* when trying to find Philippians 4:19.

Create-a-Date

Provide paper, poster board, pipe cleaners, scissors, fake fur, markers, tape, and whatever other materials you have available. Direct students to create the ideal date. Discuss questions like: "What makes him or her so attractive? What kind of character does this date have? Why does character matter? How does this date love you like God loves you? What would be God's top ten qualities in a date?"

Variations: Create the ideal parent, best friend, or ultimate reject (then discuss ways to love the reject).

Debate

Debates help students teach one another. Debates work well with issues youth are defensive about because they enable students to express beliefs from an offensive position. Debates also work well with hard-to-understand issues because they help students discover that faith can stand even with incomplete understanding. Let students search the Scriptures and draw their own conclusions with a brief informal debate. Follow these steps:

1. As students enter, direct each to draw a slip of paper from your envelope. If it says "pro," they argue for the statement, no matter how they personally feel. If it says "con," they argue against the statement, no matter how they personally feel. Debating for something they don't agree with forces students to see both sides of the issue and increases their convictions for God's truth.

2. Post the statement. Example: "Social drinking is acceptable."

3. Offer to both *pro* and *con* sides Bible passages, resources about the issue, tip sheets, and more.

4 Allow two to three minutes of preparation time (too much time leads to distraction).

5 Call on the *pro* team to speak for ninety seconds, each member speaking at least part of the time. Then call on the *con* team to speak for ninety seconds, each member speaking at least part of the time. Encourage teams to take notes while the other team speaks.

6 Using the notes, direct each team to prepare a rebuttal, using the other's points and adding further evidence for their side.

7 Call on the *con* side to present its forty-five-second rebuttal, followed by *pro*.

8 Declare open season and all-out arguing. Supplement by highlighting youth's wise statements and with points you want to make. Show how God has taught us through this process.

Dream Backpack

Give students each a paper sack, and guide them to put on the inside at least five things they think and dream about. Provide paper, markers, and other materials with which to make symbols of specific dreams. This "backpack" can be as small as a paper lunch sack or as large as a grocery bag.

Then on the outside, guide students to decorate the bag with what they show to people—one or more good habits, one or more not-so-good habits, one or more attitudes, and one or more actions. Provide the same art materials plus tape to attach the symbols to the bags.

Discuss questions like "How might your dreams be a way God communicates his plans for you (Joel 2:28)? How can you tell when a dream is from God? How do your dreams guide what you show to the people around you? When do you let actions, attitudes, and habits hide the dreams God has given you? Where can you find the courage to show people your dreams and hopes? How can you make it comfortable for others to share their dreams with you? Why is this important?"

Invite each student to add one more item to the inside and outside of their bags to remind them to let God's dreams guide their actions.

Variation: When the passage is about anger, guide youth to fill the backpacks with what makes them angry and then put on the outside how they show anger. Then talk about God's ways to manage anger. Or if you're studying loneliness, have them fill the inside with what makes them lonely and the outside with what they do about those feelings. Adapt to other assignments that match the passage you're studying.

Variation: Guide students to look in their own school backpacks to privately evaluate how what they put there glorifies or denies God. Rather than heap guilt, ask questions like "When do the notes you pass between classes encourage people? What do you need to avoid saying in those notes? How do the pictures or miniposters you put in your notebook bring attention to God or deny God? What might you add to your backpack to prompt you to treat people like Jesus treats people?"

Variation: Students could also make or use billfolds and other carry-along items.

Fold-In

Remember the feature on the back of that magazine that folds in to reveal a truth? Guide students to create similar fold-ins with both words and pictures that illustrate your Bible passage. This is one procedure that students consistently do better than their teachers. Use your Bible passage to write instructions like these:

- How can you avoid this Bible character's mistake? Fold in to see.
- Fold on the dotted lines to see how to find joy.
- Do you know what happens when you obey this command? Fold in to see.
- Fold in to see what happens when you ignore God's command to _____.

Game Creation

Chapter 5 details several learning games. Double game learning by guiding students to create the games themselves. Choose ones you can make and play in one session so the same students who create the game can profit from playing it. The exception is a review game for which students write different questions each week and then use those questions the final week. Even then the game materials could be prepared and used in play that final week.

To create a game, follow these steps:

1. Decide the game format to be used or offer two options (see chapter 5 for ideas).
2. Decide what materials and content are needed for the game. For example, Bible Trivia needs colored triangles for each team and a die covered

with matching colored squares. Its content is several questions from the Bible passage.

3. Work together to prepare the content. A team of four might divide the Bible passages into fourths and each write questions on that fourth.
4. Work together to prepare the materials. For Bible Trivia one student would cut squares for the die; one would glue them; one would cut the triangles; and one would assemble questions.

ID Card

Guide students to compose a card that verifies their identities as Christians, or as Christians who live a particular command of God. Let the words of the card grow out of the passage you are studying. Example:

I, _____, having accepted Jesus Christ am now part of a _____ people, a royal _____, a _____ nation, a people belonging to _____. Because of this I will praise God who called me out of darkness into his wonderful _____ (1 Pet. 2:9).

Signed, _____

Variation: Write certificates of adoption into God's family.

Interview Bible People

Guide students to interview Bible characters by finding their answers in the Bible and arranging interview questions to match. For Mary, students could ask, "What did you and your cousin Elizabeth talk about when you discovered both of you were carrying special babies?" (Luke 1:39–45) and "What song did you write after learning you would be the mother of Jesus?" (Luke 1:46–56). Students can then dramatize the interview, but be certain they quote from Scripture rather than speculate.

Interview Present-Day People

Send students out to people in your church to interview them about the Bible passage you are studying. Guide students to decide the questions they want to ask and to go in pairs to do the interviews. A few questions asked of several people usually works better than one long list of questions for one person. Arrange the interviews ahead so you will not interrupt a class or meeting; or do them prior to classes starting. Sample ideas:

• Invite church committee members to tell what their committees do.

- Invite a preschooler, child, teenager, young adult, median adult, and senior adult to tell what God means to them and why.
- Invite several people to teach you a tip on prayer, reconciliation, or how to do another faith action you are studying.

Variation: Collect questions about God, and then invite the pastor or other staff minister to come answer them. Let youth discover that even pastors are still learning.

Variation: Take a tape recorder while interviewing and ask permission to use it.

Variation: Interview other students (requires no prearrangement).

Inventory

Are you a shopaholic? How dateable are you? What's your friendship IQ? Students turn to these features first in magazines and newspapers. Their desire for self-understanding makes personal inventories a great Bible teaching tool. Guide students to create inventories on topics like these:

- Do you love like Jesus loves?
- How well do you show your faith to the people at your school and in your home?
- How loyal is your discipleship?

Here is a guideline to creating personal inventories:

1. Choose a topic that matches your Bible passage.
2. Guide students to create at least ten questions, each with three responses to mark such as "S = seldom," "U = usually," "M = most of the time."
3. Let the questions come directly from your Bible passage. Ephesians 4:17–32 might include these questions:

- I am sensitive to the needs of others (v. 19). S U M
- I replace deceitful desires with honorable ones (v. 22). S U M
- I use caring words rather than cutting ones (v. 29). S U M

4. Add scoring instructions. Example:

For every "seldom" give yourself one point; for every "usually" give yourself two points; for every "most of the time" give yourself three points.

1–10 points	=	I push away God's influence and choose to live in darkness.
11–15 points	=	I'm beginning to open windows for God's light.
16–20 points	=	I put off the old self sometimes, and other times I embrace my old self.

20–25 points	=	I'm letting God light up my life.
26–30 points	=	I'm walking in the light.

5. Take up the inventories, check them, and modify any damaging questions. Then direct youth to trade and score themselves. Ask, "What was your biggest surprise? What are you proud of? What will you change?"

Job Description

Older students who have filled out job applications or are deciding on a career will like this Bible study method. Guide them to write a job description based on the passage you are studying:

- Develop a job description for a Christian at your school based on Colossians 3.
- Write a job description for the Holy Spirit based on Acts 2:1–4 and John 14–16.
- Write a job description for a close relationship with God based on 2 Chronicles 7:14–16.

Learning Centers

Learning centers are self-contained learning experiences that allow students to choose what they will learn and how. They are especially valuable for studying passages that are very familiar, the we-already-know-this-why-do-we-have-to-study-it-again? passages. Students almost always discover something new with this process.

To prepare learning centers you'll need the following:

- Instruction sheets to place at each center.
- Materials to complete the instructions.
- You to circulate and encourage.

Arrange the centers in semicircles facing the wall to give each group privacy to learn. Provide a table or floor space if needed for the learning experience. Explain how to complete each learning center by holding up an instruction sheet, reading it, and demonstrating the instructions. Encourage students to complete as many centers as they can during the hour. If available, place an adult at each station to answer questions and motivate youth to stay on task.

Call everyone back to a large circle ten minutes before the session is over. Use those ten minutes to share discoveries with such questions as "What did you learn that you didn't know before? What was your favorite center and why? Who would like to show something you created at a center?"

These sample Christmas learning centers may give you ideas for creating your own:

Instructions for Center 1: Order the Facts. Next to this instruction sheet is a stack of eight cards. Each card contains an event that occurred during the first Christmas. Place these in order according to Luke 1:26–38 and Matthew 1:18–25. Then check yourself by looking at the penciled numbers on the back. (No cheating by looking early!) When you finish, scramble the cards and display them for the next person.

Materials for Center 1: Order the Facts. These facts one to a card, numbered in order in pencil on the back (display them shuffled and content up):

- Gabriel visited Mary.
- Mary was troubled.
- Mary asked how she, a virgin, could have a baby.
- The angel explained that God would be the Father of the baby.
- Mary agreed to be Jesus' mother.
- Joseph planned to quietly break off the engagement when he learned Mary was pregnant.
- Joseph had a dream.
- Joseph married Mary and waited until after Jesus' birth to have sex with her.

Instructions for Center 2: Concentration Game. Prepare a "concentration game" on the first Christmas. You will need a Bible, eight cards, and a marker.

1. Choose four facts from the Christmas story. You may study Matthew 1:18–25 or Matthew 2:1–13.
2. Write half the fact on one card and half on the other. Or write a quote on one card and the person who said it on the other. Write the Bible reference on one of those cards so answers can be checked.
3. Find someone to play your game.

Materials for Center 2: Several sets of eight cards, markers, Bibles.

Instructions for Center 3: Name the Word. Find three other people. Sit in two rows, facing each other. The person across from you is your partner. The two of you will help each other guess words from Isaiah 7:14 and 9:6. Find the Name-the-Word cards. (See **Name the Word** in chapter 5 for detail).

1. Set the Name-the-Word cards upside down on the floor between you.

2. All four of you open your Bibles to Isaiah 9:6 and put your fingers in Isaiah 7:14 so you can flip back and forth.

3. Decide who will go first. That person draws a Name-the-Word card and gives a one-word clue to the partner. If the partner guesses right, award 10 points. If not, the other team sees the password and gets a chance to give a clue and earn 9 points. Go back and forth until the word is guessed or the points are zero (each turn earns 10, then 9, 8, and so on).

4. Move on to the next word, alternating who goes first. Keep your eyes on the Bible verses to help you guess the words. (NOTE: if your translations vary, the word in the guesser's Bible is the right one).

5. Shuffle the cards after you finish and display face down for the next group.

Materials for Center 3: Paper to keep score, pencil, Bibles, four chairs facing each other, set of shuffled Name-the-Words cards with these words, one to a card: *SIGN, VIRGIN, SON, IMMANUEL, WITH, US, WONDERFUL, COUNSELOR, MIGHTY, GOD, PRINCE, PEACE.*

Instructions for Center 4: I Was There. Choose to be one of the characters at the birth of Jesus Christ. Write what you see, feel, hear, smell, taste, and think about this. You can also write your experiences in cartoon form.

Materials for Center 4: Bibles, paper, pencils.

Instructions for Center 5: Sing a Song of Christmas. Read Luke 1:26–2:20, writing down at least five facts that impress you. Choose a familiar Christmas carol, and write a new verse using the ideas you wrote down. Post your song on the wall when you finish.

Materials for Center 5: Bibles, paper, pencils, hymnals, or Christmas carol books.

Instructions for Center 6: Create a Crossword Puzzle. Read John 1:1–18, which tells the Christmas story from a different perspective. Underline key words such as *Word, beginning,* and *light.* Create a crossword puzzle on these words, using clues from the Scripture passage. Use the graph paper provided to write the words. Then copy it over with blank squares (the easiest way to do this is to put a fresh piece of graph paper on top and trace the squares). Find someone to solve your crossword puzzle.

Materials for Center 6: Bibles, graph paper, pencils with erasers.

Love in Life

Ask any teenager the goal of the Christian life and you'll hear "Love one another." Yet this is much more frequently said than done. Guide students to plan deliberate friendship with an action acrostic. For example to welcome all youth to your group, no matter what the ability or disability, youth might write this acrostic:

A *gree that we are always more alike than different.*

L *ots to give as well as receive.* We don't want to minister *to* those with special needs but welcome them to minister *with* us.

L *earn about the disability rather than believe stereotypes* (e.g., many deaf people speak rather than sign); then *Live what you know* (e.g., face your deaf friend so you can converse easily).

O *bstacles to work around.* Find ways to work around the obstacle so you can get on with God's good work, like ramp your youth room so your friends with paralyzed legs can get in too.

F *ind something in common* to build a friendship on—the same favorite author, same school subject, same hobby, same dream—and then voice that commonality.

U *nashamed to ask and do.* Don't assume you know the best way to help; ask instead, and let your friend ask you. Then once you know what your friend wants/needs/likes, do whatever it takes to communicate, to work together, to be the body of Christ. Let your friend do the same for you.

S *it together.* Friends spend time together, so put newcomers between you and an already-friend so the three of you can become friends.

Adaptation: Make love acrostics for building a group that doesn't assume one school is better than another or that one neighborhood or people group is better than another.

Manual for Christian Living

Guide students to work in teams (or a single group if your class is small) to create a manual with do's, don'ts, and how-to's for living as a Christian. Encourage students to construct their manuals according to the specific Bible passages you are studying (for a detailed example, see **Evangelism and Witnessing Booklet** in chapter 12). Here are some ideas for manuals:

- Dating manual written by guys for gals
- Dating manual written by gals for guys
- Witnessing manual containing do's, don'ts, and what-to-say's
- Explain how to travel the Roman road to salvation using Romans 3:23, 5:8, 6:23, 10:9–10, 12:1–2
- Manual on how to live the Christian life at school

- Prayer manual with pages on praise, petition, intercession, and confession
- Manual on how to keep cool in the middle of an argument
- Guide for family happiness

Maze Creation

Guide students to create mazes for each other in which the right path passes through words and actions from your passage. Wrong turns lead through results of not obeying God in the way described in your passage. Some of the turns might be marked with choices that seem right at the time but are wrong. Urge students to use illustrations as well as descriptions. Let making and traveling the mazes guide youth to talk about ways to deliberately notice right directions, how to discern hidden lies and embrace subtle truths.

Milestone Recognition

Find ways to recognize life milestones in your students' lives. This communicates that God is interested in these parts of life. Example: Give a vinyl key ring on the Sunday after each teen gets a driver's license (ask your students to remind you when a new license is granted). Before presenting the key ring and during the trickle-in time when students arrive, write the new licensee's name on the back, and let all class members initial around it with a fine-point permanent marker. Then explain to the student that you have initialed the key ring to communicate that the people in your car matter to God and that we trust you to take care of us as you drive. Don't forget to recognize these other life passages:

- *Welcome to the youth group.* Direct each student to sign a T-shirt for each seventh grader as a testimony of new friendships.
- *Middle school graduation.* Invite high schoolers to fill a bag with useful advice.
- *High school graduation.* Guide each student to voice a blessing for each senior, while you write each one down (see **Blessing** above).

Newspaper

Making newspapers can be simple or quite complex. The most effective ones with youth are those that can be completed in a single session. Cut apart pieces of newspaper-shaped paper, and give a piece to each youth on which to write an article, draw a cartoon, compose an advice column, state a want ad, or write an editorial. Let students choose the assignment that they most enjoy and work independently on it. Remind them to base it on the Bible passage you are studying, quoting from it at least once. Then reassemble the newspaper after students have completed their assignments.

Because newspapers contain so many different elements, they allow students to learn in the way that is most comfortable to them: word learners tend to choose articles, art learners may choose comics, talkers may choose advice columns, and so on.

Variation: Guide youth to investigate the passage like a newspaper reporter looking for the *who, what, when, where,* and *why.* After each student has jotted down all five, add a *how:* "How will you be different or stay committed to a current good because of this passage?"

Page-Turning Bible

Challenge students to mark a Bible with page-turning directions that help them witness or find verses on another topic. They might want to mark how to travel the Roman road to salvation using Romans 3:23, 5:8, 6:23, 10:9–10, and 12:1–2. With another color they might mark a series of Bible promises that are special to them. The markings begin on the inside cover with "Turn to page __." Then at each location, underline or highlight the verse and put "Turn to page __" for the next entry. Students decide what they want at the last page. They may be used to the joke version that ends with: "I can't believe you turned all these pages." Instead, encourage them to write something like: "Now live by the precious promises you've read." Provide topical Bibles and plenty of ideas.

Radio Show

Guide students to choose a favorite radio show or spot and use its format to present your Bible passage. Your local Christian radio station likely has some unique-to-your-area radio features. Also consider these classics:

- Hold a Top Ten radio countdown with the ten Psalms that best help today's teenagers with their problems. Discuss why these Bible songs match real life.
- Sing or read Mary's song in Luke 1:46–55 and Zechariah's song in Luke 1:67–79.
- Do a guest interview with a Bible character.
- Present a contest such as giving the most examples of how to live your passage.
- Hold a talk show, news program, or dramatic radio reading.

Talk Shows and Soap Operas

As much as we wish they didn't, students watch talk shows and soap operas. So guide students to choose these or another TV show format to present the Bible passage you're studying. For talk shows, converse about the Bible passage you're studying, asking questions that show how to live God's principles in daily life. For soap operas, demonstrate passages where God's people didn't obey God's guidance and what good they missed. Remind students to quote directly from Scripture and to deliberately present the Bible passage rather than discuss the last talk show or soap opera. Examples:

- Invite Joseph's brothers to visit your talk show and answer questions from the audience on getting along with brothers and sisters. Discuss how Bible characters are just like us.
- Create a soap opera on Abraham's relationships with his wife, Sarah, and Hagar. Discuss why loyalty to his wife would have implemented God's plan more effectively and prevented many problems.

Word Study

Some Bible words ("suffer the little children to come unto me") and illustrations ("fig tree") can be hard to understand because today we often don't use the same terms or describe life experiences in the same way. Other Bible words like *justification* and *sanctification* are packed with theological meaning. Guide students to define and study these words with such tools as a Bible concordance, Bible translations, and a Bible dictionary. Samples:

- Guide students to use **Concordance Study** (see above) to learn the meaning of the word by Bible context.
- For a verse that contains confusing words, direct students to read it in several Bible translations. Each translation will shed light on the original Hebrew and Greek.
- Direct students to look up the words in a readable Bible dictionary (or in your curriculum commentary). Choose a dictionary that is brief enough to be clear but long enough to give adequate detail such as the *Holman Student Bible Dictionary*.

After students have studied words and phrases, direct them to present the definitions in memorable form. Perhaps they'll use an object from the room to give an object lesson on that word. Maybe they'll write each word on one card and its definition on another card, shuffle them, display them face down, and play **Bible Concentration** (see chapter 5). Maybe they'll shape sanctification with a lump of clay saying, "Sanctification is letting God mold me into a happy person."

Worship Service

This project involves every student in preparing, leading, and participating in worship. As students enter, allow them to choose one of the following groups, keeping the number in each group about the same. If your class is small, let one person be a team or reduce the number of portions your service has. Spend the first three-fourths of class preparing in teams for worship and the last fourth worshiping. Remember to base all portions on the same passage. Call on teams to present their portion of worship in order: song, Scripture reading, praise, sermon, prayer. Circulate to guide teams as they work, encouraging them to complete their project step by step and asking how worship happens even during preparation. Substitute your own themes and passages:

- *Song Team*: Write an opening song for our worship experience using a familiar tune. Let your song express praise and adoration to Jesus Christ. Quote at least three times from Revelation 4:1–8:5.
- *Scripture Reading Team*: Choose phrases from Revelation 4:1–8:5 that praise and honor God. Write them in your own words or arrange verse portions. Decide whether to read responsively, in unison, or in another way to help everyone focus on God.
- *Praise Team*: Make a poster or banner that symbolizes thanksgiving, praise, and adoration of Christ. After explaining your creation, invite the group to name things they praise Jesus for.
- *Sermon Team*: Prepare a group sermon with each of you speaking one minute, based on Revelation 4:1–8:5. Include these three points:
  1. Talk about worshiping idols today. Name some we worship.
  2. Tell why these idols are easy to worship but are not worthy of worship.
  3. Spend the most time telling why Jesus Christ is worthy of worship.
- *Prayer Team*: Write a closing prayer for our worship experience. Using your own words, express ideas from Revelation 4:1–8:5. Write your prayer on large paper so we can all read it together.

Yearbook

Preparing a class yearbook takes much time but can be hugely valuable in chronicling a year of God's action. The point is for each student to keep track of the good God does in his or her life during the year; keep that goal in mind to help you know what to do and why you want all youth involved in the process. Include photographs, writings, questions to ponder, and more. Do most of this as part of your regular Bible study meetings. Let any outside work be supplemental (*don't* pick a few to work on the book, or you risk them being named the spiritual elite). Guide youth to choose a name for the book such as "Our Spiritual Journey" or another name that parallels the Bible passages you've been studying. Consider these ideas:

1. Invite all youth to take pictures all year long; you supplement by taking photos in class once a month and photos of any out-of-class activities.

2. One Sunday a month, during the application portion of your Bible study, guide each student to write an unsigned piece about what God has taught them that month and how they have lived it; even if you collect just two sentences from each student, this communicates God's ongoing work. Suggest they include line drawings if they wish.

3. Let each youth make his or her own page at the end of the year, including a favorite Scripture verse, photos, and writings they choose from those you have collected in step 2.

4. Duplicate the pages so each student may have a complete book.

Variation: Create a book in another format and for a shorter period of time. For example, each student might enjoy making a matchbook size book on prayer or a huge book with pages the size of poster board on why our God is awesome.

Plus . . .

These projects can also help your students study and understand Scripture:

• Make a slide show about the passage (use write-on slides, photo slides, more).

• Create a family tree for Jesus or another Bible character.

• Choose or produce a video that communicates the Bible theme.

• Guide students to create a "Who's Next to Whom?" scenario by giving hints about the people that you must put together to discover Bible persons' identities.

• Present book reports on books that match your passage.

• Participate in programmed learning (immediately see answers after you answer questions).

• Create a T-shirt iron-on that communicates the truth you are studying.

• Keep a notebook or journal during a multisession study.

Chapter 12

❧❧

Life Application

Experience Can Be the Best Teacher

Rationale: Jesus taught frequently through experience. The Samaritan woman experienced God's acceptance through Jesus' actions (John 4:1–26). The twelve apostles learned about ministry by ministering according to Jesus' instructions (Mark 6:7–13). The woman caught in adultery experienced forgiveness from Jesus and perhaps from many who walked away without stoning her (John 8:3–11). Peter, James, and John experienced a taste of heaven at the transfiguration (Mark 9:2–13). We teachers can provide similar life-changing experiences in Bible study by inviting youth to meet that same Jesus through the pages of God's Word.

Teaching Tip: Youth bore easily. This is frequently blamed on our quick-paced, highly visual society. But I'm convinced that youth get bored because we adults don't address the questions they have. So let them ask the hard questions like "How do we know God is even there?" Show them where in the Bible to look for the answers. Relate the Bible continually to youth's concerns such as friends, parents, worry, schoolwork, appearance, acceptance, opposite sex, love, guilt, and career. This is the essence of life application Bible study methods.

Teaching Tip: Guide youth to voice why and how Jesus' ways work. They'll take Bible application to heart when they themselves do the applying.

Teaching Tip: Thank Jesus that youth let you know when they're bored. Adults will sit politely with their minds a million miles away. Youth let you know when they're not connecting with the Bible. Let their honesty become your motivation to discover just the attitude and Bible study approaches that will help them connect to God's book so they can fall in love with him.

Teaching Tip: Whenever possible let at least one student help you write or set up the learning experience. This makes the learning truer to life and involves that student in learning through preparing.

Teaching Tip: Adults can use and enjoy almost all the methods in this book. Refuse to save the meaningful Bible study for the teenagers.

Affirmation by Name

Guide students to give and experience acceptance through affirmation. Direct each student to write his or her name vertically on paper. Instruct them to pass their papers to the left. For whoever's name they received, they are to write a Christlike characteristic of that student that starts with any one letter of that student's name. (Write the characteristic next to the letter it starts with.) Pass the papers five times. If a name runs out of letters, use a letter again. Call for the person holding the card after five passes to introduce the person on the card by reading the compliments. Return the cards to the original owners so they can keep them as an affirmation of Christ in them and as an encouragement to keep him shining. Ask, "How does it feel to have your friends notice good in you?"

Variation: While studying the names of Jesus, point out that in Bible times a person's name meant his character. Ask, "What characteristics spell Jesus? What characteristics of Jesus do you want to spell in your life?"

Variation: Let students fill out their own names to encourage them to live their faith. Their name will remind them of the qualities. Here are possible themes to go by:

- A way I can live my faith, using each letter of my name
- A way I can live reconciliation (or another action from your passage)
- How I am a part of the body of Christ (1 Cor. 12:12–13)

Variation: On the first Sunday of a new year, let students introduce each other to you via **Affirmation by Name**.

Affirmation by Secret Compliment

Give each student notebook paper and direct them to write their names in the big space at the top. Then leaving their papers in their chairs, direct them to move one chair to the left, write on the bottom line of that paper a specific something they like in the person whose name is at the top, and fold their compliment up one line so no one can read it. Direct them to move again to the left, write on the next line up a specific compliment about the person named at the top of the paper, and again fold the paper up. Repeat until everyone has a compliment or the papers are completely folded up.

Base this on a specific Bible passage, inviting students to draw upon it. For example, while studying the Ten Commandments, students would write how they see that student obey a specific commandment. Or while studying Deborah, they would write how they see this student lead others, recognizing that everyone leads through some action or attitude.

Dilemmas

Whenever you study a Bible passage that demonstrates God's problem-solving strategies, invite students to submit dilemmas they face (anonymously if they prefer). Apply the Bible strategies to solve the dilemmas. Assure students of God's power to handle whatever they face (Phil. 4:13, 19).

When discussing dilemmas, guide youth to name at least three options. The familiar story tells of a hand grenade in the room. Students may feel they have two options: (1) to throw themselves on the grenade to save their friends or (2) to let the grenade go off and kill everyone. Guide them to see a third option: throw the hand grenade out the window.

Variation: Use case studies. These are prewritten dilemmas from another person's life.

Evangelism and Witnessing Booklet

Guide students to become equipped for witnessing by preparing their own guide to becoming a Christian. Let it grow out of the evangelistic passage(s) you are studying. Consider duplicating the booklet for the church. A simple version is a piece of paper folded in half and numbered in four pages. Sample contents:

- *Cover page*: Create a cover with a symbol of new life in Christ and a Bible verse.
- *Inside page 1*: List the steps to becoming a Christian.
- *Inside page 2*: Write a prayer or prayers that someone could pray to become a Christian. Include tips for praying.
- *Back page*: Give examples of things new Christians do and don't do. Make the *do* list longer than the *don't* list (Example: Christians *do* enjoy friends who really care; Christians *don't* spend much time with friends who discourage or tempt them.)

Adaptation: Guide students to create a How-to-Witness Booklet. Include instructions like these:

- *Cover page*: Create a cover with a symbol for witnessing or questions the booklet answers.
- *Inside page 1*: Suggest Scriptures to lead someone to Christ. Include how to explain the verses.

- *Inside page 2*: Give *do's* and *don'ts* for witnessing. (Example: *Do* act natural. *Don't* act holier-than-thou.)
- *Back page*: Name excuses people give for not witnessing and ways to overcome each excuse.

Invitation to Become a Christian

The most important real-life experience is to accept Jesus Christ as Savior and Lord. Regularly offer an invitation during your Bible study. Let invitations grow out of the passages you are studying:

- When studying John 3:1–16, Romans 10:9–10, or another evangelistic passage, include all students in a time of decision with a multiple choice card or quiz. Then invite volunteers to share their decisions publicly. Your card might look like this:

  __ I want to become a Christian.

  __ I think I want to become a Christian but I have a question about

  _____ .

  __ I have become a Christian but want to obey Christ by

  _____ .

- Invite students to share ways they are growing in Christ. Ask, "How is discipleship a series of decisions rather than just one?"
- Pass out a guide that tells in steps how to become a Christian. Assign each student to one step and direct them to explain that step to the class. As students talk they learn and understand.
- Guide students to talk with God about salvation with sentence starters like these:
  - God, when I think of Jesus dying for me . . .
  - Sins I want to confess to you include . . .
  - God, knowing you love me even though I've done wrong . . .
  - God, I accept your love and salvation. Please guide my life starting with . . .
  - I'm so glad to be a part of your family because . . .
  - I want my life to be different by . . .
- Emphasize present benefits (security, peace, advice) as well as future ones (heaven rather than hell) so youth won't want to put off salvation.
- Invite students to give 10- to 30-second testimonies on why they are Christians or would like to become Christians. Lead a time of prayer inviting any who have not become Christians to do so.

Close with delight over those who have accepted Jesus during this hour. Encourage them to make their decision public during the next church worship service. Offer to go with them when they do so. Encourage all students to live their commitment to Christ, whether made now or in the past.

Magazine Accounts

Youth love to read about how other teenagers live the Bible. So subscribe to Christian youth magazines that provide true-to-life testimonies written about everyday teenagers just like them (limit stories about famous heroes since youth may assume they can never do what they do). Bring these articles in when they match the Bible passage you are studying. After reading the article, invite each youth to write two paragraphs on how they have lived or could live the Bible passage.

Adaptation: Invite your class to write the personal accounts without the magazine jump start as in **Profile Story** in chapter 7.

Adaptation: Show youth how to subscribe to Christian youth magazines so they can benefit from their true-to-life articles daily.

Month-long Habit Making

Caution kids against assuming that reading their Bibles and obeying God is easy. That's why they're called spiritual disciplines. Refuse to motivate with "if-you-were-a-good-Christian-you'd-do-this" tactics. Instead show your students how to develop Christian habits. Popularized as the Forty Day Test, this process says to make yourself do a certain something every day for a month to six weeks. It then becomes part of your routine—it has become a good habit. Remind students that Jesus chose the habit of going to the synagogue weekly (Luke 4:16). Ask what habits Jesus would recommend we choose. Encourage students to prompt and nag each other for a month on disciplines such as these:

- Read your Bible for five minutes at the beginning of homework.
- Pray while you take your shower.
- Say an encouraging word to everyone you see.

When students miss a day they may become discouraged; insist that they not declare their thirty days a failure but start fresh the next day picking up where they left off.

Motto for Life

Based upon the Bible passage you are studying, guide students to declare a life motto. Here are some examples:

- Ephesians 4:29: "Compliments, not cuts" or "Use loving words, not sarcasm."
- 1 Thessalonians 5:17: "Jesus is my steering wheel, not a spare tire."
- Psalm 23: "God will get me through anything."

Multiple-Choice Sharing

This method invites students to compare themselves to a Bible character or experience. Each question or sentence fragment is followed by several options, plus a blank line for students who prefer to write their own responses. In small groups, each student answers the first question and tells why they answered as they did. Then all move to the next question. Such sharing promotes empathy (sharing the feelings of another) and the realization that we all have similar experiences. This sample examines Cain and Abel (Gen. 4:1–16):

1. I'm like Cain because
   a. I'm an older child in my family.
   b. I neglect to bring my best to God.
   c. I feel like killing my brother/sister sometimes.
   d. I act nice when I have evil intentions.
   e. _____

2. I'm like Abel because
   a. I'm a younger child in my family.
   b. I bring my best to God.
   c. I have been attacked by my brother/sister.
   d. I don't always notice evil intentions.
   e. _____

3. After I've done wrong like Cain did, I
   a. avoid God's questions.
   b. avoid God.
   c. try to get away with what I have done.
   d. complain that life is not fair.
   e. _____

4. When God and I talk about sin I
   a. try to talk him out of punishing me.

b. find myself amazed that he still cares.

c. move away from the people I have hurt.

d. move away from God.

e. _____

5. Sin builds upon sin. A sin I have let build is

   a. jealousy, which led to revenge, which led to the end of a relationship.

   b. lying, which led to more lying and covering up so that I destroyed trust.

   c. deception, which led to hurting someone, which led to denying it.

   d. avoiding God, which led to feeling distant from him.

   e. _____

6. A way I will stop a sin from building is to

   a. go ahead and confess it when I first notice it.

   b. ask a parent or another adult I trust to help me recognize sin patterns.

   c. turn back around rather than assume I must keep doing the sin.

   d. ask someone to show me how to stop a sin.

   e. _____

Multiple Endings

When discussing ethical issues, guide your group to work together to write a story with multiple endings, similar to the once popular choose-your-own-mystery books. This extracreative procedure may take most of the Bible study time but guides students to experience decision making and consequences of decisions before they actually make those decisions. Suggest that each ending be the result of a certain choice or series of choices and that both good and bad consequences be true to life. Suggest also that readers be allowed to turn around at several points in the decision process, to communicate that we can start making good decisions even after we've made bad ones.

Discuss by inviting students to share tips for anticipating the results of decisions before making them. Deuteronomy 30:19–20 goes well with this procedure.

Prayer Dialogue

Guide each student to write a prayer dialogue beginning with his or her words and writing what he or she understands God to say back. You may want to give guidance during the prayer like this: "Talk with God about your current friendships. What does he like? Write a line from you and then a line from God, a line from you and then a line from God. [Pause while youth write.] What does he want you to change in your friendships? Write a line from you and then a line from God, a line from you and then a line from God. [Pause while youth write.] How does pleasing God in your friendships make both you and your friends happy? Write a line from you and then a line from God, a line from you and then a line from God."

Variation: Write a dialogue between God and a Bible character.

Pretend You Are There

Guide students to prepare to live the passage you are studying by pretending they are experiencing what the Bible characters experienced. Students may focus better if they close their eyes. Try out these possibilities:

- Pretend you are in the room praying for Peter while I read to you about Peter knocking to say he has been set free. What are you thinking? feeling? doing? What do you say to Peter (Acts 12:5–17)?
- Pretend you have just died. Where are you going now? What does heaven look like? What does Jesus say to you when you meet him? What do you say to him? What questions do you ask him? What emotions do you experience (John 14:1–3; Rev. 21)?
- Pretend you have just died. What are people saying about you? What do they miss about you? How did you impact their lives? Open your eyes and write your own obituary or epitaph and three ways you could make it come true (Eph. 5:15 and Col. 3:1–17).
- Pretend you are riding in a car with your best friend. Another car runs a red light and smashes into yours. When you come to, you realize your friend is not moving. You feel for a pulse, but there is none. How do you live the truths in Philippians 4:13, 19 and 1 Thessalonians 4:13–18?
- Pretend the day you have been looking for has arrived. Jesus has returned. What are you doing when he comes? What is he saying and doing? What else is going on (Mark 13)?

Quiet-Time Sparks

Quiet time, that time alone when we read the Bible and pray, is not the only time we spend with God. Instead it is the pilot light that gets the fire burning for the whole day. Encourage your students to think of their "time with God" as the full twenty-four hours. Invite them to name ways to get the fire burning and then let that fire of devotion burn twenty-four hours a day, seven days a week. Examples:

- Speak words Jesus would speak—let your quiet time give you ideas.

- Show interest in what people say with responses like "Tell me about it . . ." instead of "So!" Watch the Bible for ways Jesus showed interest in people.
- Think of a way to bring a smile to every person you meet; notice actions and attitudes that do this as you read your Bible, and then ask God to show you how to do them.
- Deliberately speak in a calm voice when you are aggravated to show God's power. Notice the way Jesus did this in Matthew 4.

Say It Aloud

Students tend to believe and do what they say. So coach them to say, "Inappropriate!" when they're watching a movie and an ugly use of language or an ugly treatment of a person appears. Coach them to say, "In marriage only" when a sex scene occurs. And when violence appears, coach them to say, "Treasure people." These simple phrases help students deliberately see good and bad. They can benefit from the good of the movie by filtering out the added junk. And when they need to turn off or fast-forward a movie, they'll know why.

Sensory Learning

Because the more the senses are involved, the longer the learning lasts, ponder ways to use all five senses as students learn. (Some studies show that smell produces the longest memory.) Start with these possibilities:

- *Smell*: Noah's ark, sweet savor of prayer, Lazarus' death, Jonah in the fish
- *Taste*: Figs, loaves and fishes, salt of the world, manna, milk, meat
- *Hearing*: Noises as the Jews left Egypt, the children laughing on Jesus' knee, people of all ages rejoicing as Jesus entered Jerusalem
- *Sight*: Eyes of people who encountered Jesus, dusty feet that Jesus tenderly cleansed, the faces of Simeon and Anna when baby Jesus entered the temple
- *Touch*: Crown of thorns, weight of burdens, acceptance hugs

Setups

Set up a situation before students enter to help them experience that day's Bible passage. Examples:

- Lay a student volunteer on the table and cover him or her with a sheet. Coach this student to lie perfectly still. As the other students enter, ask, "Is this person dead? How can you tell?" The person may begin to giggle when others poke at her. Point out that though she may pretend to be dead she cannot be dead unless she really is. What qualities would she need to be dead? How do you know the person is alive? Follow by studying spiritual life and death with a passage like Romans 6:1–8.

- Invite an adult whom students do not know to pose as a vacant-eyed homeless person, to ask for their shoes, and more. When they don't give them, he could leave the room defeated and saying, "I knew this love-your-neighbor stuff was all talk."
- Invite a friend from another community to pose as a new student who is very shy or dresses differently. Notice the way students relate to him. Follow with a study on Luke 14:1–14 or James 2:1–13.
- Pack everyone into a small room without a window. Turn out the lights and study passages like 1 John 1–2 (living in the light), John 11:1–44 (Lazarus raised from death), Acts 12:1–11 (Peter's escape from prison), or a passage detailing Paul's imprisonment.

Spiritual Gift Saying

Avoid the too-frequent tragedy of assuming that those who speak up in class are the leaders or the gifted. The Bible clearly says that every Christian is gifted and every Christian is a critical part of the family of God. Besides that, the talkers may enjoy the focus on themselves a little too much. So openly recognize the good in each student by voicing each student's spiritual gifts and guiding classmates to do so with a process like this:

1. While studying spiritual gifts in passages like Romans 12, 1 Corinthians 12, and Ephesians 4, invite each student to privately write down three gifts they think they might have. Give three cards for this.
2. Then give each student a card, call the name of the student whose birthday is closest to today, and direct the group to write down the spiritual gift they see in this person and one expression of it. For someone with the gift of prophecy students might write, "You don't mind saying what's right even when you're the first to speak up." Collect those cards and mark them with that student's name.
3. Repeat for every other student.
4. Then distribute the cards to their owners. Say, "Sometimes the people around you see good in you that you don't see. Other times you haven't shown them good you know is inside. Let your affirmation and theirs combine to let you play with God's full deck."

Spiritual Gift Showing

Each time an application step comes, ask questions like "How would someone with the spiritual gift of mercy apply this passage?" "How would those with the gift of prophecy speak this truth?" Guide youth to continually voice ways all spiritual gifts act in everyday life. In casual settings use sentences like these: "I like the way you showed hospitality by helping Shelley feel at home." "You showed encouragement by prompting him to answer —and he was right!"

Trust Walk

This method is so old that it's new. Blindfold one student, and instruct a partner to lead this student through a path loaded with obstacles. Inside obstacles could be chairs and walls. Outside obstacles could be tree branches and potholes. The idea is for the leader to show protection and gentle guidance for the blindfolded one. Possible applications include:

- How easy was it to trust the one who led you? How were these experiences like or unlike trusting God?
- How easy was it to lead someone who was totally dependent on you? What implications does this have for the way we treat other people, even those just getting to know us?
- What would have happened if the one leading you abused your trust? How can you tell whether guidance is from God or from Satan, who wants to hurt you?
- When is it time to show the exact way, and when is it time to give general directions?

Variation: Let a quiet voice give directions among a cacophony of distractions (if you have a hard-of-hearing member let them give the directions rather than be unable to hear them). Let the application be on how to hear God's still, small voice.

Variation: Let several give directions, some reliable and some not. Invite students to voice how to tell the difference between good and destructive advice (such as learning the voice that gave good advice before).

Video Creation

Creating and watching a video takes considerable time, but the effects can be memorable. Types include:

- *Training video*: Prepare a series of role plays that show right and wrong ways to witness, to make friends, to comfort someone during crisis, or whatever your theme. Base these on the Scripture passages you are studying.

- *Bible memory verse charades*: Make certain verses memorable by acting them out phrase by phrase and filming them.
- *Retreat video*: Guide students to video selected discussions, simulations, recreation, and testimonies during your youth event. Then enjoy reliving those moments. Many have no sound except for background music that's added. Guide students to avoid all hints of embarrassing each other.
- *Music video*: Make a **Music Video** with Scripture points set to music (see chapter 10).

Write Your Own Ending

Direct students to write a new ending to the Bible story. Let this be an opportunity to benefit from the Bible character's mistake without having to make that mistake. For example, what if David had resisted sleeping with Bathsheba? Stress that youth cannot change Scripture but they can think through ways to change their own wrongdoing before it happens and can deliberately choose to do the right thing.

Plus . . .

Try these other options for applying Bible passages to life:
- Simulate other cultures.
- Take a mission trip to learn about missions (start in your own community).
- Love in real life by sending cards, inviting to come along, including, and more.
- Write a will telling what you'll leave to whom and why.
- Write a will naming nonmaterial things you'll leave to whom and why.
- Hold a Quaker meeting, which is silent until someone feels led to speak.
- Present a mock trial: "If you were arrested for Christianity (or a specific element of it), what evidence would convict you?"
- Create and recite a litany of praise.
- Sign each other's papers to remind each other that we all belong to Christ's family.
- Name all the problems we don't have when we follow Jesus Christ.

Chapter 13

❧❦

Bible Memory Joggers

Remember tomorrow what you studied today.

Rationale: "I have hidden your word in my heart that I might not sin against you" (Ps. 119:11).

My students say they can't memorize.

We try Scripture memory, but the kids say it is boring.

Bible memory doesn't have to be hard or boring. And teenagers *can* memorize—they do it every day. They memorize the words to radio songs, telephone numbers of friends, answers to the next test, and more. Use these skills to memorize the Bible. Then guide youth to live what they memorize.

Teaching Tip: After each Bible memory experience, help students understand it by asking, "How did this help you memorize the verse? How will you live what you memorized?"

Accountability

One reason we don't memorize Scripture is because we don't get to tell anyone we've done it. So pair students to congratulate each other's successes and to persist through working out the verse portions they haven't yet memorized. Guide accountability partners to exchange phone numbers and call each other at midweek to recite for each other. Take time during class to check on each other as well. Let each pairing last about a week. Then re-pair.

Acrostic

Challenge students to organize the Bible verse in phrases so it spells a word. It can be a real word or a nonsense word; the point is to let the letters of the word prompt students to remember what comes next. This example uses a nonsense word: HATLAM (hat a lamb wears):

H e has showed you, O man, what is good.

A nd what does the LORD require of you?

T o act justly and to

L ove mercy

A nd to walk humbly with your God.

M icah 6:8

Card by Card

Write each word to the Bible passage on a separate card. For long passages, write phrases on the cards. There are different ways to use the cards:

- *Unscramble:* Shuffle the cards, and challenge youth to place them in the correct order, looking at their Bibles for verification.
- *Unscramble to beat the clock:* Time youth the first time they unscramble the cards. Then challenge them to unscramble more quickly the second time, and then the third.
- *Elimination:* Once the cards are in order, direct students to repeat the verse a couple of times. Then remove a key word, and challenge youth to repeat the verse, filling in the word, from memory. Continue removing words and repeating until the verse is memorized.
- *Elimination with choice:* Let youth take turns choosing key words to remove, as they memorize through elimination.

Credit Card

Explain that God's Word is valuable and a reminder of it deserves to be kept with our other valuables. Distribute credit-card size papers (white poster board works well) and markers. Guide students to write out and illustrate the memory verse. Urge students to keep this "credit" in their billfolds or wallets to remind them to use it. Ask, "How is counting on the truth in this Bible passage similar to the way you count on a credit card? Different?"

Jigsaw Puzzle Assembly

Guide youth to create jigsaw puzzles to help them memorize the Bible verse. Have each student write the Bible passage on paper, cut the paper into a set number of jigsaw shapes, and then trade to let another student assemble it. In the process youth will memorize the Bible passage and reference. Important: use jigsaw shapes.

Locker Poster

Guide youth to make a locker-size poster of the Bible memory verse, decorating it with illustrations, doodles, and borders. Writing and decorating the verse sets it in students' minds. Each time they open their locker, they again remember the words to the verse. Other types of posters include

- posters that fit the corner of a bathroom mirror;
- billfold-size posters;
- full-size poster board; and
- **Doorknob Poster** (see chapter 7).

Memory by Rhythm

Guide students to memorize Bible verses or truths by setting them to a rhythm, musical tune, or rap pattern. Invite one preenlisted student to start the rhythm. Prompt others to join in, and then gradually add the words to the tune, reading from Bibles for the words. Repeat until the words smoothly fit the rhythm, and until volunteers can say the verse from memory.

Note: This is an excellent way for a student who may be new to the Bible and to church to participate. If he or she has musical talent, invite him or her to start the rhythm or rap. This student then becomes the leader in a familiar area and becomes open to the Bible.

Memory by Voice

Good-naturedly explain that though it's seldom easy to memorize an entire verse, memorizing one or two words is easy. Assign to each student one word or phrase from the Bible verse you want to memorize. Direct students to recite their words in order, each one saying only his or her assigned word(s). Do this several times, and then challenge volunteers to recite as much of the passage as they can by looking at each classmate and saying their word(s). Point out that they memorized the entire verse by hearing each other say individual words.

Memory Where You Are

Divide students into trios, and challenge them to list more places than any other team where they can memorize Scripture by repeating it. Offer these ideas to start their thoughts flowing: in the shower, in a traffic jam, while waiting for the orthodontist, between homework assignments, while getting dressed, by adding another verse to a song they're thinking about. Urge students to discover ways to connect Scripture memory to what they already do.

Prompt each youth to pick one place to keep flash cards of the verses your group is currently memorizing. Make the flash cards during this session.

Missing Vowels

The Hebrew language had no vowels. Guide youth to read and remember Bible passages by printing them in English without vowels. As they struggle to pronounce the words without the vowels they will remember them. Example for Romans 12:1:

"Thrfr, I rg y, brthrs, n vw f Gd's mrcy, t ffr yr bds s lvng scrfcs, hly nd plsng t Gd—ths s yr sprtl ct f wrshp."

Picture Is Worth a Thousand Words

Invite students to doodle or draw a single picture of the Bible verse. They can use symbols, illustrations, and more. Then instruct them to recite the verse using the clues in the picture. For example, Psalm 119:11 ("I have hidden your word in my heart that I might not sin against you.") might be a large heart with WORD hiding in one of the folds with a sign with SIN crossed out. Point out how visual images make the verse easier to remember.

Guide youth to trade and solve each other's pictures.

Proclaim

Guide students to speak the verse to each other using the tones and volume that would best help people remember it. Some verses will invite quiet tones, others more boisterous tones. Because they've spoken the verse, they'll remember. Because they've heard the verse from a peer, they'll remember.

Puzzle Cubes

Memorize six related verses at once by writing one-fourth of each verse on a square card and taping the cards to six different sides of four blocks. Students arrange the blocks with the correct side up and in proper order. Seeing the verse segments during arranging helps them memorize all six verses.

Rebus

Encourage each team to draw a rebus of a Bible memory verse for the other team(s). A rebus changes words to pictures. Examples: The word *be* becomes a honeybee. The word *for* becomes the number *4*. The word *sing* is drawn with open-mouthed choir boys. Words like *the* might be left as is. Divide your class into two or more teams of one or more persons each, using a dividing method from chapter 16. Direct them to change each word to a picture. A sample rebus:

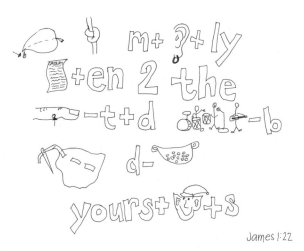

James 1:22

Recorded Scripture

Many Bible verses have been recorded word for word by Christian musicians. Play these when they match the Bible passage you're studying. The tune helps teens remember the verses.

Other recorded Scripture is spoken rather than sung. Students can listen to either while driving, while getting ready for school or work, or while completing a project.

Refrigerator Magnet

Guide students to write and decorate the memory verse on a small paper. Then back it with magnetic tape so students can display it on their refrigerators, in their lockers, or on another magnetic surface.

School Cheer

Guide students to develop a cheer or cheers based on the verse(s) to be memorized. Ideally, the cheers should repeat the verse word for word. The best process is to choose a school cheer, write it with a blank line after each phrase, and then write the Bible verse on the blank lines, matching the cheer syllable by syllable. Work in teams of two to three to write and sing cheers. See chapter 16 for team-forming methods.

Scrambled Letters

Scramble the letters within each word of a Bible verse. Challenge students to unscramble them. This detail work results in remembering each word.

Variation: Scramble the word order within verses and challenge students to put the words in order.

Scrambled Standing

Write each word to the passage on a separate card. Give one card to each student. Direct them to stand and to arrange themselves so the words show in correct order. Time them to see how long it takes. *Hint*: Youth may stand exactly backwards, forgetting the perspective of the reader. If this happens, laugh along and urge youth to try again.

Collect and shuffle the cards, redistribute them, and challenge youth to do it in less time than before. Repeat once more. Each time, youth will remember more phrases and how they go together. Recite the verse together, and then call on individuals to recite it.

Teaching Tape

Guide students to make their own teaching tape, imitating language teaching tapes. Prompt youth to take turns saying each phrase of the Bible verse into a tape recorder. After each phrase is spoken, leave a silent space on the tape that is long enough for the listener to repeat that phrase. Finally, guide youth to record the entire verse in unison and to allow silent space to repeat.

Play the tape back and invite the entire group to repeat each phrase during the blank segments. Duplicate one copy of the tape for every youth. They can then play the tape while in the car or while preparing for the day.

Adaptation: If you have a large group, guide them to work in teams with separate tape recorders to record different verses related to the Bible passage you're studying. Then exchange tapes to play and repeat.

Translation Comparison

Invite students to read the memory verse from several Bible translations (the Bibles youth bring usually provide variety). Ask volunteers to share the wordings they like best and why. Continue with questions such as "Which words really bring out the meaning of this verse?" As students discuss the verse, its truth will take root in their hearts.

As they talk about different translations, remind students that the Bible was written in both Hebrew (O.T.) and Greek (N.T.), so we all read from translations. Reading from several translations is one of the best ways to understand the meaning of a verse, and thus to remember it.

Tunes

Guide students to choose a tune they like and sing a Bible verse to it. These tunes can be commercial jingles, hymns, self-composed music, or contemporary songs. Write the original words syllable by syllable and substitute the Bible verse words. Sing as a group repeatedly until it is memorized.

Write-offs

Writing the verse impacts memory more than saying it because writing involves the eyes and hands, rather than just the voice. Invite students to generate ideas to make "write-offs" fun rather than a punishment. Here are some ideas to start:

- Race to do "write-offs" faster than any other team, each team writing the verse a specific number of times.
- Write the verse with right hand and then left, with cursive and then with print, seeing how many different ways you can make each line look.
- Ask each student to write a copy of the verse for every other member of the class. Do this on postcards. Then mail one card to each youth each day. This gives each member a postcard from every other member and that many reminders to memorize the Bible verse. The writers will remember the verse because they wrote it. The receivers will remember the verse again when they read it.

Plus . . .

These methods, detailed in other chapters, are also excellent Bible memory methods:

- **Footprint Reading** (chapter 4)
- **Limerick** except use Bible verses word for word (chapter 7)
- **Letter Maze** (chapter 7)
- **Name the Word** (chapter 5)
- **Trading Game**—use for verses with lists such as the fruits of the Spirit, Ten Commandments, twelve tribes/sons of Jacob, more (chapter 5)
- **Maze Creation** (chapter 11)
- **Letter Board** (chapter 5)
- **Bible Concentration** (chapter 5)
- **Decoding** (chapter 7)
- **Telephone Numbers** (chapter 7)
- **Crossword Grid** (chapter 7)
- **Charades** (chapter 9)

Part 3

Put It All Together

Chapter 14

❦

Work the Bugs out of Your Teaching

Teaching youth gets better with practice, understanding,
and training.

Q: *Why do I have to use youth involvement methods? Why not just tell the*
kids about the Bible and how to live it? I can fit more Bible study in if
we don't take time for all this fun stuff.

A: Use involvement methods mainly because Jesus did. He lectured very
seldom—the Sermon on the Mount is his one long talk recorded in the
Bible. Most of the time he used question-and-answer, listening, parable
(story), and other people-involving teaching methods (see chapter 1).

Second, use methods because it's quite easy for your students to let your
telling go in one ear and out the other. Students can smile and "be good"
but not learn a thing. The more involved they are with the Bible, the
more they'll remember the Bible and the more they'll live what they
learned.

Third, use methods because involvement with the Bible guides teenagers to trust and obey God. The reason why you can "fit more Bible study
in" when you talk is because you're summarizing the results of hours of
your own Bible study. You are the one who has grown—not the kids.
But when kids dig into their own Bibles, they have "aha" moments
where the Bible comes alive for them, just like it did for you. They meet
God as they study his Word. Let them have this privilege.

Recall the mountain climbing illustration at the end of chapter 1: Taking
teens to the top takes more time than saying, "The results are worth the
climb." But the climb changes students' lives. Guide students to experience the exhilaration of discovering God's truth in the Bible, the joy

of putting into practice a truth they discovered, and the delight of personally summarizing a week of walking with Jesus.

Q: *I agree that students need to study the Bible for themselves, but mine just aren't motivated. Why bother trying if they don't want to learn?*

A: Because the Bible has the answers they're looking for. Youth may not seem interested in the Bible, but they're very interested in relationships, and what does this mean, and does anybody care if I live or die? Because the Author of the Bible has the answers to these questions, we cheat youth when we refuse to provide them the Bible study that leads them to these answers. You can lead a horse to water and then you can make him drink if you feed him enough salt. So until youth are old enough to attach meaning to Bible learning, feed them methods that make them hungry for God's Word. Provide a Bible learning game that hooks their interest, and then give an assignment that leads them to just the solution they've been seeking. Chapters 4–13 show you how to let the methods connect kids with the Bible.

Q: *So how do I motivate them?*

A: As you well know, youth won't come to you openly motivated to learn, but they will grow motivated as you take the time to show them how to encounter and live the Bible. The Bible says "Whoever believes in him will not be disappointed" (Rom. 9:33 GNB). Keeping this in mind, focus on four elements of good motivation:

Meaningful

Moves toward the Bible

involve   **M**ovement

use the   **M**outh

Guide your students toward **M**eaningful Bible study by relating it to their lives. Show students how **M**oving toward the Bible answers their questions and gives them the happiness they seek. Students learn better when some part of them is **M**oving to shape righteousness or take their place in a learning game—especially on a sleepy Sunday morning or during a nighttime Bible study after a long day in school. Finally, because students remember what they themselves say, give opportunity for students to use their **M**ouths.

Q: *If I do all this fancy stuff, I won't have time for the Bible study. How can I fit it all in?*

A: The "fancy" stuff *is* the Bible study. Notice that a good Bible method gets teenagers looking at and learning from their Bibles. **Bible Tic-Tac-Toe** may seem like a mere game, but during it students must read their Bibles for answers. During these repeated readings they learn Bible facts. Then they can use those Bible facts to write a diary entry on how to resist temptation at school. The Bible has become a part of their lives, not just an intellectual encounter.

Q: *I try to get my students to talk by asking questions, but they just sit there or one person answers all the questions.*

A: Because it's risky to answer questions, many youth won't venture it. Even the school-smart may not know their Bibles as well as their math. And those who do talk may do so in a selfish way that keeps center stage for themselves. Equalize talking, and make talking about Scripture inviting to all your students by using methods that require everyone to speak. When everyone talks, no one feels "on the spot." Possibilities include:

- **Under Chair Questions** (chapter 6)
- Many variations of **Talk around the Circle** (chapter 6)
- **Bible Jeopardy** (chapter 5)
- **Hot Bag** (chapter 6)
- **Agree/Disagree** (chapter 8)

Second, welcome *every* answer students give. Without meaning to, you may give more attention to a few youth, assuming they are more serious about Bible study. But even the quietest youth has great insights. And those who speak frequently may act quite carnally once class is over. When any student ventures, welcome contributions warmly with "Brilliant!" or "Thanks for that idea!" or "Beautiful Bible understanding." Then prompt them to move past churchy answers with "How will you help that youth feel welcome at church once you invite him?" and "With what attitude would you show that forgiveness?" Even totally off-the-wall answers can be welcomed with "Tell me more" and "What verse led you to that conclusion?" As students sense that you really want to hear what they have to say, they'll speak up. Refuse to believe that some students are happy being quiet.

Finally, make it safe to talk about the Bible (see next question).

Q: *My students talk just fine until I ask a question about the Bible. Then no one will say a word, and I end up doing all the talking. Why won't my students talk about the Bible?*

A: Talking about ball games and school is easy because youth have had lots of practice. Make talking about the Bible just as easy by giving Bible-talking practice. Help youth feel safe and smart, so they can discover how to be spiritual.

First, refuse to answer your own question. You've been thinking about it ever since you started preparing. Your students need a little time to think about it. Let silence prompt them to speak. If they don't get the answer after a bit, rephrase the question. Show them the verse, then the line, then the word, until they get it. Give them practice looking in their own Bibles to voice their own answers.

Once you've asked a student a question, never move on to someone else. That student needs the Bible encounter of finding the answer for themselves. They can do it because the Bible's answers are available to everyone. If another student tries to answer for them, tease them with, "Wow! How did you make your answer come out of her mouth? Great ventriloquism! Now make it come out of your mouth." When that teen voices the answer, he gains confidence in reading and understanding the Bible.

When students answer incorrectly, point out the part of the answer that was right, and then prompt them on to the rest of the answer: "Paul was not one of the original twelve disciples, but he was a disciple in the way every Christian is a disciple. So you were partly right. Try looking in the last few verses of the chapter."

Finally, enforce the "no-slam" rule (see chapter 2). Youth need to know that what they say in class will make sense to others, and that nobody will make fun of them for talking. Help this happen by forbidding any cutting: "In this class we listen to each other and value each other. I will not allow cuts or sarcasm." As you become the heavy, students learn the treasuring habit from you. Then make absolutely certain that you use no slams or put-downs. We Christians can give each other a bit of heaven right here—a place where we experience the treasuring love of our Lord through people who genuinely want to hear what we have to say.

Q: *I passed out play clay and asked my students to shape forgiveness. They just looked at me and said, "You've got to be kidding! We aren't children anymore. Why do we have to do this dumb stuff?"*

A: Youth worry intensely about looking dumb in front of their friends. Even when they'd enjoy shaping clay, they hold back for fear of looking babyish. Your enthusiasm is the key to overcoming this resistance. If you say, "Well, the book says we have to do it . . ." your students won't like it. But your students will feel free to dig deeply into spiritual truth when you genuinely say, "Forgiveness is such a difficult concept to grasp, that together we can understand it. As each of you makes a symbol of forgiveness, we'll all understand it better." If your group still resists, say something like "Humor me and try it. Your ideas always impress me, and I look forward to hearing them." Most students enjoy what the teacher enjoys. Paper and pencil is not more mature than play clay or drawing. In fact, high school seniors are the ones who enjoy clay shaping the most—and use it to voice the deepest spiritual insights.

Q: *No matter what I do, my teenagers just won't quit talking. They have to share their romance stories, details about the ball games, and more.*

A: See these distractions as opportunities. Few youth come to Bible study sessions ready to focus on the Bible passage of the day. Rather than scold your students for this, let the Bible passage invite youth to discover God's answers to the needs they're already talking about. For example, when the lesson is on God's wrath, and your students are intent on discussing a rumor at school, use the rumor to show how God's wrath works. Point out that one aspect of God's wrath is letting us have the consequences of our actions. Ask these questions: "What consequence will come as this rumor spreads? What are the reasons behind the rumor? *revenge? pride?* What does God advise? How are people obeying or ignoring this advice? Who will be hurt or helped by these choices? What will you do?"

Listen to what youth are talking about, and use a question or two that moves your student right into the day's Bible lesson. This becomes easier as you notice that you must do the same thing. As you walk into a worship service that you did not plan, you must move from current thoughts and worries to focus on God and his solutions to those thoughts and worries. Help your students do the same.

Q: *Again and again this book suggests leaving the Bible open during quiz-zes, games, and other Bible learning activities. My students get all the answers right that way. If the kids are always looking in their Bibles, when are they going to remember the stuff on their own?*

A: When they leave class. Finding the right answers is exactly the point. We're not in Bible study to test youth's knowledge of the Bible, but to give them opportunity to learn something new from it. As they keep the Bible open they study it, understand it, and discover why they can trust the Bible for everyday guidance. The hour you teach is the time youth open and study their Bibles with intensity. Let them learn inside class. Then prompt them to keep reading at home. Keep kids' noses in the Bibles for these reasons:

- The Bible is the source of answers. We want them to have lots of experience noticing that.
- The more success youth have with getting Bible answers right, the more confident they'll feel about their own Bible skills, and the more they'll read and heed the Bible outside of class.
- We're in Bible study to teach students the Bible, not to prove them wrong. Students get plenty of experience with failure outside church; they don't need to cope with doses of it at church too. Yes, this is different from the world, but we're not of this world.
- When students do fail to correctly identify a Bible truth, lead them to the answer so they can see that the Bible helps them redeem mistakes.

Q: *Why go to all the trouble to create a learning game? Why not just ask the questions in discussion format?*

A: It does seem more trouble, but learning games can be as simple as drawing a baseball diamond on the chalkboard or arranging four chairs. Games don't have to be complex, but they tend to be effective. The trouble is worth it for many reasons :

- In discussions, one or two people tend to answer all the questions. Learning games invite participation from every student.
- Some students will be there because their parents made them come. They have little, if any, interest in spiritual things. But their spiritual interest is stirred when they are pulled into the game. As they play, they discover the Bible has the answers they've been looking for.

- Learning games give shyer kids a chance to talk and gives kids who don't do well with traditional learning methods a chance to shine by doing the game skillfully.
- Moving encourages attention. Students are sleepy on Sunday mornings. If their bodies are moving, their brains can't go to sleep. The game itself invites attention and motivates students to dig in their Bibles.

Q: *My students never bring their Bibles. How can we do Bible study without Bibles?*

A: You can't. So keep department Bibles, all the while motivating students to bring their own. It's almost a rite of passage that youth in seventh grade stop bringing Bibles. There are ways you can encourage them to bring and read from their own Bibles:

- Use them frequently. Even the most spiritually focused teenagers will leave their Bibles at home if they're not used in class.
- Guide youth to mark their Bibles during the study to enhance home study. Marking Bibles makes youth want their own Bible rather than the department extras.
- Quietly slip a small candy every week to each student who brings a Bible. For those who don't bring one say, "I know you'll bring it next week." Don't fuss. Don't pronounce the Bible bringers as more spiritual. Just give a sweet reward for a sweet action. This is not bribery—it's motivating students until they are ready to motivate themselves. And it's praise for a job well done. I have senior boys come back to my ninth-grade class to show me they brought their Bibles and to ask for their candy. It's not the candy they want as much as my knowing they remembered their Bible.

Do keep extra Bibles in readable translations for students who do not bring their own. Studying God's Word is more important than whose name is on the inside cover. As comfort with the Bible increases, students will more readily bring their own Bibles.

Q: *I tried a method in this book, and it flopped. What did I do wrong?*

A: Possibly nothing. Some weeks, whatever we try flops. The experiences the students have had before arriving, the peers who are there or not there, and the particular mix of the group affect Bible study. These tips may decrease your flop rate:

- Talk to other teachers to find out how they use that method. As with a recipe, they can give you tried-and-true tips.
- Focus on the students. Let them do most of the doing, talking, creating, and reporting. Openly cherish every one of them. When you like them and like their contributions, they'll study the Bible more fervently.
- Establish firm rules for the learning games right up front. Changing rules frustrates and angers kids. They want games to be absolutely fair.
- Enjoy the activity yourself. If you like it, the youth probably will.
- Plan for more than you need. Then if an activity flops, you have an alternate plan.
- Practice the activity with another teacher ahead of time. If you have weekly workers' meetings, this is a great time to give ideas a trial run.
- Reread an activity that flopped to decide how to alter it next time. Do you need more specific instructions? More consistent care for your students? Did the method not match the type of Scripture passage you had?

Q: *I'm not creative enough to try all these fancy methods. What can I do that's safe for me?*

A: The only truly creative person is God himself. He works through each of us to impart his creativity to others. Those who look more creative have just had practice in letting God work. So go ahead and let him work through you. See creativity as a type of courage—courage to try something new for the sake of your students' learning. I'm woefully inadequate in drama, so I frequently skip steps that use it. But one week when I could think of nothing else, I was forced to use skits. I discovered that my students loved drama and put complex spiritual truth into understandable form through it.

   To expand your creativity, scan a chapter that interests you and try one of the methods in that chapter. Try just one new method at a time to give yourself time to feel comfortable with it. Step by step you can do it. Why? Because God is your guide.

Q: *My students get all nervous when I ask them to be creative in their writing or their other assignments.*

A: Don't say the term. Because the word *creative* threatens many students, use phrases like "put your ideas on paper" or "choose your own words." If you use the word *creative,* explain that it means "choosing for yourself what you will say, rather than letting someone else decide for you."

Q: *My students are too mature for these creative methods. How can I be sure we stay with the more deeply serious stuff that they say they want?*

A: Amazingly, an activity like clay shaping can bring out some of the most profound spiritual truths you will ever encounter. Teenagers are awesome in their discoveries and presentations; they simply need a vehicle through which to do it. Those who really want serious stuff will get serious with any method.

Your students may have had a parent or teacher who insisted that the only "serious" Bible study is "sit down and listen." While not contradicting these persons, note the many ways Jesus taught (see chapter 1), and show them to your students. Then explain that mere talking makes it easy to say the spiritual thing but not do the spiritual thing. A variety of methods prompts students to live spiritually rather than just talk about it.

Refuse to stay on the surface with any group of teenagers. It also helps to explain the purpose of each method. For example, when using the **Agree/Disagree** (chapter 8) talking method, explain to your students that this is not for sharing opinions but for discovering every side of God's multifaceted truth. Repeat before, during, and after the learning experiences how students have delved into seriously understanding, and deeply living, the Bible.

Q: *I feel like I bore the kids. They don't seem to pay much attention. How can I become more interesting to them?*

A: The best cure for boredom is meaningful Bible study applied to the students' lives. Part of that cure is letting youth discover that meaning for themselves. So let your students talk. Guide them to voice how each passage impacts their lives, answers a question, or gives them power. Your voice will prompt this process, but their voices will take the majority of the hour. Their voice might come through talking, writing, doodling, drawing, and more. Your church's curriculum should help with how to do this week to week. Some tips:

1. *Stop talking.* In your eagerness to give your students the answers, you cheat them out of the delight of discovery. One reason people go to sleep during lectures is the speaker does all the talking—and thus the learning. So let your times of talk be brief, and with the goal of inviting your class to participate. Use a little silence to prompt them to contribute. Chapter 8 offers ideas.

2. *Vary your methods.* The worst Bible learning method is the one you use all the time. So vary your methods—there are over three hundred options in this book. Then notice which methods invite the most Bible focus from your students and use those again.

3. *Invite students' help.* Telephone a student and ask which of two possible learning methods he prefers. Ask another to draw a rebus to put under the concentration game. Invite another to lead a small group, providing directions. Keep a checklist to make certain you call on every youth within a certain period of time. Participation helps students "own" the study and motivates them to make it work.

Q: *How do I find time for studying my lesson?*

A: To find time to prepare, set a regular time during the week, and keep it just like you would any other appointment. Adjust the time until you find a set time you can keep weekly: before work, after work, while waiting for a child to finish a practice or a lesson, during lunch break, or on the bus. You may want to add a review time after your main study. See chapter 15 for five steps to lesson preparation that spell R.E.A.D.Y.

Q: *I'd love to try all these interesting methods, but I just don't have time to get them all ready. If I just talk, I don't have to make all the visuals and prepare all the experiences.*

A: Preparing to guide students to study the Bible for themselves usually takes about the same time as studying for a lecture, sometimes less time. Begin in the same way by studying the Bible yourself so you understand the passage. But then focus your time on preparing to guide students rather than deciding what you'll say. Decide a method for each of the four basics: read the Bible, discover Bible facts, understand Bible facts, and apply Bible facts. Consider the preparation needed for this combination, compared to what it would take to prepare an hour-long lecture:

1. *Read the Bible:* In script form using the Bible as your script (chapter 4). Preparation: None, besides bringing extra Bibles.

2. *Discover Bible facts:* Pairs of students find five Bible facts, create a **Bible Concentration** fact match game (chapter 5), trade and play to reinforce the facts. Preparation: Get markers and ten cards for each pair of youth.

3. *Understand Bible facts:* Students write **Letters** home about the events in the passage from the perspective of one of the characters

(chapter 7). Preparation: Get paper and pencils, list characters in the Bible passage.

4. *Apply Bible facts:* Students choose one of the facts they wrote in the **Bible Concentration** game (chapter 5) and make a **30-Second Speech** about how that truth can impact their lives (chapter 8). Preparation: None.

Note: Lecture can be an involvement method. Just don't overuse or let it go longer than five minutes. Remember: a good Bible teaching method doesn't entertain youth; it guides them to discover Bible answers for themselves. Entertaining youth can be just as boring and meaningless as lecturing to them.

Chapter 15

❦

Tips For Youth Bible Study Preparation

Whether you're using curriculum or starting from scratch, this R.E.A.D.Y. acrostic summarizes five basic steps for Bible study preparation:

R ead the passage first and jot down what God says to you through that passage. Your God-given insight is valuable along with that of the teacher who wrote the curriculum.

E xamine the Bible passage by using the commentary material in your curriculum or by using other Bible commentaries and articles.

A sk Jesus to show you how he would communicate this Bible passage and assess the needs of your youth. How would he answer your youth's questions? How would he meet the needs they have expressed recently? Seek methods that make the application of the Bible passage obvious.

D ecide which methods you will use. Choose about four methods: one that motivates youth to *read the passage*, one that guides them to *examine Bible facts*, one that guides youth to *understand the facts*, and one that guides them to *apply the facts* to their lives (see p. 199–200).

Y ou open and close with a specific verse or point. What is the one Bible truth you want your class to remember? Repeat it during the session, let your methods demonstrate it, and emphasize it at the end.

Bathe all the above steps in prayer and a request for the Holy Spirit's guidance. As John 16:5–15 explains, the Holy Spirit is the One who convicts, guides, and makes Bible truth clear.

Chapter 16

❧❧

Thirty-Two Ways to Form Teams

Tired of "1-2, 1-2"? Use a different method each time you form teams or divide into smaller groups. Teams allow students to bridge friendships they might not otherwise try. Varying the team formation weekly allows students to build the whole-group closeness they yearn for. Initially students may balk at the unfamiliarity, but later they look forward to each new way you divide them.

Hint #1: Rather than just posting the dividing method, ask students the characteristics as they enter — "What's the last digit of your phone number?" — and send them to that group. This helps students understand the division method right away and speeds up the process.

Hint #2: When a student brings a friend for the first time, keep them in the same group.

Hint #3: Make the size of your teams match the assignment to keep a few students from doing the work while the others watch.

Hint #4: The purpose of teams is to pool ideas and resources to give each other security and ability. Verbally affirm this every time you see it happen. Prompt the true teamwork that calls on all students rather than encourages a few to shine.

1. Last Digit of Phone Number

Direct students to think of the last digit in their phone number and put them in groups accordingly. For five groups, the first group is everyone whose phone numbers end in 1 or 2, the second group is those with phone numbers ending in 3 or 4 and so on. For two groups use odd/even; for ten groups use one for each number; and so on.

Advantages: Students want to know each other's phone numbers. They may pay close attention to this information, and to each other, as they divide into groups.

Disadvantages: Groups must be a factor of ten. Groups may be uneven. If this happens, divide by next to last digit.

2. Birth Month

Divide students into two, three, four, six, or twelve groups by birth month. For three groups, you could divide into those born in January–April, May–August, and September–December.

Advantages: Youth are usually proud of their birthday. This also gives opportunity for lighthearted competition, like "People born in April are smartest!"

Disadvantages: Students born earlier in the year will be more mature and at an advantage in some kinds of study processes. Defeat this maturity advantage by grouping January with July, February with August, and so on. Also some months may have more students born in it than others. If this occurs, shuffle by actual birth date, moving the latter portion of April to the May group, etc.

3. Birth Day

Gather everyone who was born the first through fifth day of the month on one team, everyone born the sixth through tenth on another, and so on for six teams. Divide into ten teams, five teams, three teams, or two teams similarly.

Advantages: This gives a less often recognized characteristic in common than birth month gives. Each month that day rolls around, students can remember some who were born on or near the same day of the month they were.

Disadvantage: Teams may not divide evenly. Overcome this disadvantage by moving according to the hour born.

4. Jawbreakers

Give students jawbreakers with multiple layers of color to suck on. At group time, direct students to stick out their tongues. Divide by tongue color.

Advantages: This is neutral and fun. Students won't suspect the candy as the dividing method (at least the first time).

Disadvantage: Really big jawbreakers bend or pull off braces brackets. Use smaller ones and caution all students not to bite them.

5. Favorite School Subject

As students enter, ask them their favorite school subject. Send them to the circle with the label that matches. For five groups you might name Math, Science, Reading, Foreign Language, and Social Studies. Then if a student says "English," pair her with the reading group.

Advantage: When kids who like math sit with other kids who like math, they no longer believe that liking math is weird. This builds bonds between students.

Disadvantage: Students may sit in a circle just to be with a friend. Overcome this by asking individuals their favorite school subject first and then sending them to a circle.

6. Number of Letters in Name

Gather students whose names have two or three letters in one group, those with four letters in another group, those with five letters in another group, and those with six or more letters in a final group. One time gather according to first name length, another time gather according to last name length, and a third time gather according to middle name length.

Advantage: For many students there's no sweeter sound than their own name. So when students group according to it, they feel a special happiness.

Disadvantage: Some students feel embarrassed about their middle name or even their first name. Your vocal valuing of each name will reduce this disadvantage.

7. Hair Color

Direct the students to stand in one long line, arranging themselves from light hair to dark hair. Group A is the first four students in line, group B the second four, and so on. Each foursome has similar hair color.

Advantage: You can give complements about each student's hair.

Disadvantages: Some people think blondes have more fun, brunettes are smarter, and so on. Debunk these myths by highlighting something good that each youth says in the learning process. Some students may feel uncomfortable having their hair color pointed out.

8. Favorite Sport

Post above every gathering of chairs the name of a sport that the students play or watch. As students enter, ask them their favorite sport and send them to that group. Vary this by one week asking the sport they like to *play* and the next week asking the sport they like to *watch*. Sports include soccer, swimming, wrestling, volleyball, track, baseball, basketball, football, tennis, rugby, and many more. You might name all ball sports one week, and then one-on-one sports the next week.

Advantages: This can provide another bond for students, show the strength in a variety of sports, and help students know that their sport is significant.

Disadvantage: Some students won't have a clear favorite. They might enjoy coming up with one, however.

9. *Favorite National Team*

Always avoid pitting local school against local school, but do occasionally divide by national teams. Choose hockey leagues one time, baseball leagues another, basketball leagues occasionally, and so on. The national loyalties aren't as biting as middle school and high school loyalties. But if you do notice the same destructiveness, don't repeat this method. Dividing methods are meant to form bonds, not pit person against person. At all cost, avoid praying for certain teams to win or asking God to bless one team over another.

Advantage: Many students spend a great deal of time keeping up with sports heroes and teams. This grouping affirms this often-healthy pursuit.

Disadvantage: Too much sports interest keeps students from developing other interests.

10. *Puzzle Piece*

Cut paper into the same number of pieces as people you want in a group. Distribute the pieces, and direct students to find others who complete their puzzle. If you cut several different puzzles, the puzzle pieces that match will be the ones that make a group. If you cut several copies of the same puzzle, you can match according to color, or ask that students find someone of each different color to complete the puzzle.

Advantage: This grouping develops students' mingling skills as they find their groups. It also affirms puzzle workers.

Disadvantage: It takes extra time to cut puzzles.

11. *Shoes*

Direct students to look at the shoes they are wearing and join the shoes-that-buckle group, the shoes-that-tie group, or the shoes-that-slip-on group. More shoe groups include two sets of eyelets, three sets of eyelets, four sets of eyelets, and so on. In the summer sandals could be divided by buckle, slip-on, or Velcro.

Advantage: Especially among older students, shoes are a neutral way to divide into groups. Do avoid this method if your students are into brand-name shoes for status.

Disadvantage: Middle school students may feel self-conscious about the size or style of their shoes.

12. Tickets

Give students a ticket as they enter (any rectangle of paper). Or place the tickets under chairs before they arrive. When group time comes, assign students to groups by color of ticket. To prevent ticket exchanging, give both various shapes and colors so students don't know the dividing method. Or form groups with one of each color rather than same colors.

Advantages: Easy to do; many variations. Tickets don't have to be elaborate and can be made at the last minute. For the under-chair variation, students don't know the ticket is there until after they sit down.

Disadvantages: Takes time to tape all the tickets under all the chairs. Students who are handed tickets quickly figure out that tickets are the matching method and may exchange tickets to get in certain groups. Vary the way tickets are matched to overcome this disadvantage.

13. Class against Class

If you have more than one youth class, announce an end-of-the-session competition. This motivates classes to study hard in preparation for the competition. Group games like **Bible Jeopardy** work well for this (see chapter 5).

Advantages: This promotes a team feeling in each class. It encourages cooperation to excel. Finally, it builds a bond between teacher and students when the teacher coaches and takes pride in her class.

Disadvantages: If wins are overemphasized, or losses are handled poorly by leaders, one class may feel superior or inferior to the others. One class may be older or smarter than the other. Work hard to keep the competition friendly.

14. Pencils

Pass out pencils. Divide into groups by the color of pencil or length of pencil. Consider letting students line up their pencils in order of length and then dividing the line.

Advantage: Students won't think of pencils as a group maker.

Disadvantage: You may not have different colored pencils or pencils in various lengths.

15. Colored Paper

Distribute paper for your assignment in a variety of colors. Direct students to gather with others of their same color, or with one of each color. Consider different shapes as well so students don't know how you're going to group.

Advantages: Little preparation is needed since you bring paper for the Bible study assignment anyway. It also can be varied each time it is used.

Disadvantage: Your team activity may not require paper.

16. Marked Paper

On the back of the paper or worksheets students will use, mark a number. When the time comes to form groups, direct students to look on the back of the worksheet to find their group number.

Advantage: The surprise element is the greatest advantage. At least the first time, students don't expect the worksheet to be a vehicle for dividing into groups. After they figure this out, you can create different markings and groupings. For example all the odd numbers gather rather than all the 1's. Letters that spell names in your Bible passage can also become group-forming strategies.

Disadvantage: It takes time to mark the papers.

17. Color of Eyes

Place the blue-eyed students in one group, the brown-eyed in another, and the green and hazel in another group. If uneven, shuffle by shade.

Advantages: Most students are proud of their eye color and may develop closeness with someone of the same eye color. It gives a chance to notice and give eye compliments that are independent of color such as "loving eyes," "expressive eyes," "spunky eyes," "happy eyes." Consider working this into your Bible study process.

Disadvantages: There may be more of one eye color than another. Some students may not like the color of their eyes. Some students may feel self-conscious if their eyes aren't the "standard." Complimenting each set of eyes may change the way students view their eyes, turning it to an advantage.

18. Chair Arrangement

Cluster your chairs the way you want students to group. If you need four groups of six, cluster the chairs in four circles of six chairs. If you want each student to talk to one other student, set two rows of chairs that face each other but have space between each chair. If you want students to talk to one person at a time, set up two circles, one inside the other, with the inside circle facing the outside circle—students can talk with the one across from them, move to the left and talk to the next person, and so on.

Advantages: Students group themselves as they enter. This can give them freedom to choose while still accomplishing a teaching goal.

Disadvantage: Students may move the chairs. Avoid this by circulating and explaining the reason for the chair groupings.

19. Note in Balloons

Write numbers on small white paper and insert them in uninflated balloons. Direct students to blow them up and shake to read the number through the balloon.

Variation: Students blow and pop the balloons to read their number.

Advantage: Balloons add intrigue and color.

Disadvantages: Students might get distracted by playing with balloons. It also makes a grand mess, can be loud, and takes time to prepare.

20. Color of Clothes

As students gather, look to discover two or three color groups in what the students are wearing and divide by those. For example, gather one group by blue and green; a second group by red and brown. Vary by using shirt or dress color one time, shoe color the next, pants color the next.

Advantage: Students enjoy being noticed for what they wear.

Disadvantages: Everyone may be wearing the same color. More may be wearing one color than any other color. If so, divide by shade.

21. Cross to Another Grade

If your group has students in more than one grade, direct each eighth grader to find a seventh grader, and so on. Give the directions to the older grade to develop leadership. This can grow even easier by setting one circle of chairs inside another and explaining that older grades sit on the outside circle and younger grades on the inside circle.

Advantages: Students tend to stay in their own grade. This forced crossing keeps students from feeling like a baby if they talk to someone younger. They discover that similarities are greater than differences. They form the friendships they've been wanting.

Disadvantage: Some will be cruel to younger ones, or obnoxious to older ones. Close supervision prevents these tragedies.

22. Family Groups

Assemble groups with one student from each grade. Let the twelfth grader lead one time, the seventh grader one time, the eleventh grader one time and so on. Stress that *each* youth can be a leader, but don't just tell them to lead. Show them how with a list of three questions and attitudes that encourage groups to talk.

Advantages: Hearing Scripture truth from the viewpoint of every age group gives a multifaceted picture of Scripture. Students learn from each other. Students realize that Christ is the one who unites us, not school or grade.

Disadvantage: Conversation will not come naturally at first, because some students have little experience with talking to those outside their grades; show students how to patiently bridge these gaps. Some topics are best for older students and some for younger students. So use this dividing method when you're discussing topics that apply to all ages.

23. Shoe Size

Instruct students to recall their shoe size. Direct the odd sizes to one group, even to another, and half sizes to a third. Do not tell shoe size. Divide by odd/even rather than by large/small to avoid self-consciousness.

Advantage: Allows for private response.

Disadvantages: Students with big feet may feel self-conscious about it. You might make big feet important or desired by making them group captains. Also, kids can "cheat" if they don't have to tell their shoe size.

24. All Say an Animal Sound

Write several animal names on your chalkboard. Challenge students to choose one, make the sound the animal makes, and find other animals of the same kind. Vary this by saying they must form a "barnyard group"—one of each kind of animal in each group. Or assign animals to the students before they enter the room to keep things even. This dividing method is best before a team assignment that is active and in a room setting that won't disturb other classes.

Advantages: It's fun. It permits students to be silly with a purpose. It relieves energy that can then be channeled for Bible study.

Disadvantages: It's noisy. Groups may form unevenly; balance groups by physically moving some to other groups, or by assigning one to be a horse, one to be a chicken, and one to be a cow, before assigning another to be a horse.

25. Candy

Distribute any kind of candy with a variety of colors. Direct all the oranges to get together, all the yellows together, and so on. Another time gather two reds with two oranges, two yellows with two greens, and so on. Still another time, gather one of each color in your group. Changing the gathering method keeps students from choosing a certain color to be in a certain group.

Advantages: Students like candy. Candy is familiar.

Disadvantage: Some candy pulls off braces brackets. Choose candies that won't do this so the braced students in your group won't have to turn down your candy gift.

26. Guy-Girls

Put the guys on one team and the girls on another.

Advantages: Can demonstrate that guys are as smart as girls and vice versa. Can keep public displays of affection from distracting players. Separates couples.

Disadvantage: You may have more girls than boys or vice versa.

27. Divide the Room

Divide students into groups according to where they are sitting. The left half of the group becomes one group and the right another.

Advantage: This is especially good for discussions and assignments that require much comfort, because students usually sit next to people they feel comfortable with.

Disadvantage: Some friendships are counterproductive to good Bible study. One who must impress another may hesitate to share a weakness. Two who try to out-macho each other may refuse to participate.

28. If You Have ...

Divide those who have done their homework from those who have not. Divide those who have tests the first half of the week from those who have them the last half of the week. Divide those who have little brothers and sisters from those who do not. Choose different characteristics each time you use this gathering method. And *always* choose distinctions that create bonds rather than put-downs.

Advantages: This helps students see each other's similarities. Students will come to Bible study wondering what you'll think of next. It's unusual and fun.

Disadvantage: Groups may not divide evenly.

29. By Subject or Option

If your study includes several options, allow students to choose their group according to interest. For example, a study about guy-girl relationships might include a group on dating, a group on how to know if you're in love, a group on how to get someone to notice you, a group on breaking up, and so on. Or any Bible study might include the option to write a poem about the passage, draw a picture of the passage, say a paragraph about the passage, or create a model that illustrates the passage.

Advantage: This allows students to learn in a way that meets a felt need.

Disadvantage: Students may choose what their friends choose rather than what they really want. This can be overcome by highlighting something good in every group.

30. Odd/Even

Whether dividing by day of birth, birth month, last digit of phone number, or number of letters in a name, let the odd numbers go on one team and the even on the other side.

Advantage: You can tout the advantages of being odd or even to the matching group.

Disadvantage: You can only form two groups this way.

31. Alphabetical Street

Form groups by the alphabetical order of the street names where the students live. Combinations are endless: The A's and Z's could form a group, the A's through G's, and tons more.

Advantage: Helps youth learn one another's street name.

Disadvantage: May not divide evenly by letter, but adjustments can be easily made by moving to the second letter.

32. Choose Your Own Group

From time to time, encourage students to choose their own groups. Do this after you've tried most of the other dividing methods and students have formed bonds across age, grade, school, and other people-dividers.

Advantages: When students choose their own groups they continue friendships and affirm the students they choose to be with. Those who are chosen feel accepted.

Disadvantages: When students choose, they might limit themselves to certain friends. Some may not get chosen and may feel unacceptable. Some matches are distracting or destructive.

Important: Under no circumstances should you allow a few students to choose teams. No matter how it is done, someone is chosen last and that person hurts. All students should feel loved and accepted at church. Refuse to set up a situation that will cause one youth to feel rejected.

Chapter 17

꒰Ꙭ꒱

Thirty Ways to Make Announcements

Announcements happen every week. Keep your kids listening by varying the way you communicate:

1. On the Floor

Write your announcements, one to a page, and display them across the floor.

2. In the Door

Cover the entire door opening with paper. Write your announcements on it. Attach it at the top only so students won't break the paper as they come through.

Variation: Tape the door after students are in the room. Allow students to break through on their way out.

3. On/From the Ceiling

Youth's eyes continually wander to the ceiling. Take advantage of this by placing announcements there. Vary them by hanging some posters from the ceiling on masking tape strips at various heights.

4. On E-mail

Enlist all students to tell you their E-mail address. Then send mass E-mails to communicate. Don't form an E-mail clique by failing to get the information to those without E-mail—use telephone, mail, or whatever works best for that teenager.

5. On Banners

Enlist students with computers to make announcement banners. These students not only become crucial to your group, but they remember the announcements they printed. Call on every youth to do this; those without computers may want to use a friend's computer or hand letter them. Encourage students to vary the way they design and display the banners to maintain interest: horizontal, vertical, upside down.

6. On Youth

Let students "wear" announcements as hats, notes on backs, notes on noses, or the old-fashioned "sandwich boards."

7. Guess the Announcement

Many announcements are standard ("youth choir this afternoon at 4:00"), and students know what they are. But guessing reminds them.

8. Maps with Details

Write your announcement directly on a hand-drawn map to the location. With the map dominant, write details in the corners including beginning time, ending time, cost if any, what to bring, and the address and phone numbers.

9. Coded Messages

Send a postcard with the announcement in code or give the announcement in code as students arrive. The fun of unscrambling focuses students' attention on the content. Samples: If you're announcing a new Bible study series, scramble the titles. If you want youth to save money for the coming retreat, make a treasure map with details about the retreat. If someone's birthday is coming, code the date and age.

10. Answering Machine

Invest in an answering machine for the church or your home and set it on announce only. When students call they'll get a different message each week that conveys announcements as well as a Bible verse that offers a spiritual growth tip. You might want to set it to take messages as well as give announcements. Students could then let you know if they're coming to the event, tell you a prayer request, or say what's on their minds.

11. Singing Commercial

Enlist each week a different team of students to compose and sing a commercial that includes all your announcements. Spontaneity keeps most students from getting nervous, but some students would rather practice a day or so ahead of time. Suggest that students write a new verse to a current commercial or compose their own jingle. Highlight something good in every team's presentation, and keep a list to deliberately involve all students. Even if they hesitate they'll enjoy taking part in some way.

12. Postcards

With your copy machine or computer printer, prepare a unique postcard for each event. It doesn't have to be fancy—just changing from a white postcard to a blue one will invite students' attention. For Bible studies intrigue them with a question the Bible study will answer. Or give partial answers for which students can find the fill-ins during the sessions. For events, include all the details students need in order to get to the event and back home again.

13. Newsletters

Most students love receiving their own mail. Mail or distribute a regular newsletter that contains coming events, a challenge to live the Bible truth you're studying, little-known facts about your passage, and more. Invite students to help you compose and arrange these, again pulling on different teams at different times. Keep a list to make certain you draw on all students equally.

14. Footprints

Write one word to a footprint, and let students enjoy walking on them as they read.

15. Sealed Orders

Make a big deal of saying that only certain people will get to hear a particular announcement. These people are of course the ones whom the announcement pertains to. Perhaps they are the nursery workers for that day after Bible study, and you're reminding them. Or the junior high-ers have an event this week, and you're reminding them. The next week the senior highers will get the information, and two different nursery workers will be notified. The secrecy makes all youth want to know. If youth don't discover it, communicate later that those who heard were those whom the announcement pertained to.

16. Word of Mouth

This is the old-fashioned "telephone" game. With students seated in a long line or circle, whisper the announcement to the person on one end, who whispers to the next, and so on. Ask the one at the other end to recite it, and the one who began the message to confirm or correct it. Shuffle positions, and send the next announcement down the line. If you have a hearing-impaired member, let him start the message or read lips when his turn comes.

17. Find Out Who

Tell a few students about the event, making certain you tell different students every week (keep a list). This makes students want to find out who knows the scoop. Also, as students tell others, that convinces the group that "everybody" is going.

Important: Never assume that if you've told a few students, all students will know. They may say they've told "everybody," but that means they've told the ones they know best. For critical information, back this up with another announcement method such as postcards or mass E-mail.

18. Tape Recorder

Each student plays the announcements as they enter. Make it more intriguing by varying the voice from week to week. They'll have as much fun guessing the voice as they will listening to the announcements.

19. Scavenger Hunt

Put one announcement at each discovery location. See **Walk and Find** in chapter 6 for sample locations. Two samples:

- Announcement #1 is on the ceiling.

  Don't forget to bring your Bible next week.

  Look for your next announcement under a table.

- Announcement #2: Next week bring an object lesson that tells about faith.

  Look for your next announcement by the chalkboard.

20. Peek-and-View Box

Amazingly, teenagers love this one. Attach announcements inside the box in a font large enough to read. Cut two eye holes and slits for light.

21. Different Youth

Invite a different youth to give the announcement each week. Encourage them to communicate with great enthusiasm. Varying the voice invites attention. Keep a list to make certain you call on *every* youth. If students don't want to talk, they can make posters, etc.

22. Doorknob Hangers

Draw a doorknob hanger shape. Write or type the announcements on it, then duplicate it, cut it, and pass it out. Put one on the doorknob of your classroom, deliver them to youth homes, or distribute and direct students to hang them on their bedroom doors at home. Especially helpful for a series of dates students must remember such as the meetings for teaching Bible school.

23. Photographs

Display photographs of the last Bible study activity. Seeing what a good time the group had motivates others to come. Pass the photographs with the date, time, and place on the back. *Never* use embarrassing photographs, and *always* privately ask students if you can display any picture with him or her in it.

Adaptation: Prepare a poster with the photographs and details. Hang the poster in a place where students will notice it.

24. Skit

Guide two or more students to prepare and present a skit that communicates one or more announcements.

25. Printed Pencils or Balloons

If your event is several weeks away, order pencils, balloons, or other "printables" printed with the date, time, place, and purpose.

26. T-shirt

Print T-shirts prior to the retreat or other big Bible study event, and require students to wear them as admission. Distributing the shirts ahead of time generates excitement for the event.

27. Buttons

Use a button maker, blank stickers, or white name tags cut in the shape of your theme. Write the details on them. Distribute and wear them.

28. Puzzle

Print announcements on paper, cut them into 4 to 6 jigsaw pieces, and direct students to assemble them. Your computer software may have a program that does this. Students can rotate in small groups to assemble each announcement puzzle.

29. Bulletin Board

Let students read announcements on the youth bulletin board. Rotate announcements regularly. Even better, style the bulletin board like a calendar, and post announcements on the day that matches. Students can add prayer requests and other announcements.

30. Birthdays

Though this is not a technique, announcing birthdays should be a part of every week. Keep a chronological list of students' birthdays, and weekly note who has a birthday coming. Sing, hug, or otherwise congratulate these people at the beginning of your Bible study.

Chapter 18

꿰

A Dozen Ways to Group Your Chairs

Variety makes learning intriguing. So just as you vary any other teaching factor, vary your chair arrangements. Students will come in wondering how the chairs will be arranged and how that arrangement will point them toward Scripture. Here are twelve of the endless possibilities:

1. Circle within a Circle

Face the inside circle out and the outside circle in, so students sit facing a partner to discuss a Bible verse. You can move students to their left periodically to give new partners.

2. Knee to Knee

Arrange chairs in twos or fours so students sit facing each other, knee to knee. Because students are in close proximity, they can feel comfortable telling Bible discoveries and what those mean to them. This is good for **Multiple Choice Sharing** (see chapter 12).

3. Around Tables

Tables can give the group a family feeling. It also provides a surface to complete a group **Doodle Sheet** as in chapter 9 (cover the table with white paper), a poster, or other project.

4. Shape of Your Theme

If you're studying witnessing, arrange your chairs in a W to remind students that we sometimes travel a long time (the height of the W) before we get to points of witnessing (the three places the W changes direction). Or if you're studying temptation, arrange the chairs as obstacles that students must bypass to get to the doughnuts. Invite youth to help you discover room arrangements that communicate the theme.

5. No Chairs

When leading an activity like **Agree/Disagree** (see chapter 8), take out all of the chairs. This helps students feel freer to move and avoids sitting rather than participating.

6. One Large Circle

Use this when you want everyone to hear what everyone else says. Good for hearing-impaired students who read lips. This arrangement is also good for **Talk around the Circle**, during which everyone gives an answer different from everyone else's answer (see chapter 6).

7. Small Groups

Arrange circles of chairs for the number of groups you want. Choose the number of groups by assignment: If your passage has five key points, assign a grouping of verses to each of the five different groups. See chapter 16 for thirty-two ways to form small groups.

8. Learning Centers

Arrange chairs in semicircles facing the wall to form centers where smaller groups of students will work on a specific Bible learning activity. See **Learning Centers** in chapter 11 for ideas. One center might be a quiz game in which students learn Bible facts. Another might be a place where students put those facts into a poem or song. A third center might guide students to write a letter explaining the passage to someone without a church background. Learning centers are especially fun at Christmas, Easter, and for passages that students assume "I-know-this-stuff-already-because-I-study-it-every-holiday." The learning center approach takes students deeper in their understanding and application.

9. Triangle or Square

When studying the trinity, seat your chairs in a triangle to remind youth of the Father, Son, and Holy Spirit. Perhaps each side will find characteristics of that expression of the trinity. Or put your chairs in a square to talk about ways we box in God or let the world box us in. Think of any variation on the circle and how it might communicate the passage you're studying.

10. Game Board

You'll set up three rows of two for a game called **Row**, where students move forward one chair each time they get a correct answer. The first one to answer correctly from the front chair wins a point. You use three rows of three for **Human Tic-Tac-Toe**. (See chapter 5 for these and other games.)

11. Panel

A row of experts sits across the front, while the rest of the students sit in a semicircle, or rows, facing them. These experts could be students themselves, parents, church staff members, or whatever the unique group that meets that subject's learning need.

12. Premier Seating Only If Plentiful

Avoid the use of couches or other premier seating unless there is enough for everyone. This avoids one group of students getting the comfort that others don't have. Or declaring that their spot. Or fighting for seats. Or starting turf battles. Each of these divides youth from youth—the opposite of building the body of Christ. Students may laugh and say they don't care, but they do.

Index

See a method in your curriculum you're not sure how to do? Remember a method from this book but can't remember what page it's on? This alphabetical listing of methods and topics helps you find both. Seed ideas are listed by name only, but their chapters offer tips for leading them.